Better Homes and Gardens.

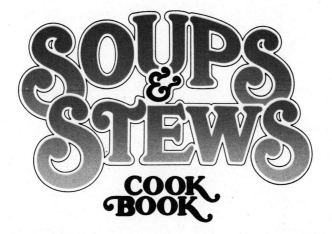

© 1978 by Meredith Corporation, Des Moines, Iowa
All Rights Reserved. Printed in the United States of America.
First Edition, Third Printing, 1979.
Library of Congress Catalog Card Number: 78-56642
ISBN: 0-696-00445-3

On the Cover: Delectable *Cioppino*
is a California seafood stew you can
easily prepare using canned and frozen
seafood. (See recipe on page 73.)

BETTER HOMES AND GARDENS BOOKS

Editor: Gerald Knox
Art Director: Ernest Shelton
Associate Art Director: Randall Yontz
Production and Copy Editors:
David Kirchner   Paul S. Kitzke
Soups and Stews Cook Book Editor:
Flora Szatkowski, Associate Food Editor
Food Editor: Doris Eby
Senior Associate Food Editor: Sharyl Heiken
Senior Food Editors:
Sandra Granseth   Elizabeth Woolever
Associate Food Editors:
Diane Nelson   Patricia Teberg
Recipe Development Editor: Marion Viall
Soups and Stews Cook Book Designer:
Sheryl Veenschoten
Senior Graphic Designer: Harijs Priekulis
Graphic Designers:
Faith Berven   Linda Ford
Richard Lewis   Neoma Alt West

Our seal assures you that every recipe in the
Soups and Stews Cook Book is endorsed by the
Better Homes and Gardens Test Kitchen.
Each recipe is tested for family appeal,
practicality, and deliciousness.

Contents

Satisfying Soups and Stews

The truly special flavor and aroma of a homemade soup or stew is always welcome. Whether you choose a delicate broth or a thick and meaty bean soup, a spectacular wine and seafood stew or a nourishing vegetable soup, it's an eating experience you'll enjoy.

Prepare a soup or stew for any part of the meal. In Meal-Mate Soups, you'll find first-course soups, and soups that turn a sandwich or salad into a meal. Some sweet cold soups even double as dessert or a treat for breakfast or brunch. And any of these can make a lively snack—a cold one when the temperature rises, or a hot one for a chilly day.

If you're looking for a main dish, leaf through Whole-Meal Soups and Stews. These stand alone; complete the meal with a salad and bread or crackers.

The last section of the book is a guide to Soup-Making Basics. Here you'll learn how easy it is to make a long-simmering stock from scratch. Also included are recipes for noodles, dumplings, crackers, and croutons—the extras that make your home-made soups and stews special.

Of course, you needn't spend all day in the kitchen to make a satisfying soup. Commercial products combine with fresh ingredients to make delicious soups in a hurry. Such recipes are grouped on the pages labeled Quick Soups. They're perfect for busy cooks.

A soup or stew is a lot more than a side dish to eat with a sand-wich. Whether you're preparing an appetizer or a dessert, a special din-ner for company or a quick lunch for the kids, you'll find all the soups and stews you need in this book.

MEAL-MATE SOUPS
hot & cold soups

When you need a soup to complete a meal, choose from those in this chapter. Sample clear broths, creamy chowders, and chilly soups for appetizers that fit a variety of menus and serving styles—from very casual to very elegant.

A steaming bowl of soup, particularly one with vegetables or meat and vegetables, completes a sandwich or main-dish salad meal.

Serve cold soups according to their character. All are appropriate as first courses or snacks, and cold fruit soups can be intriguing desserts, as well.

Meal-mate soups include (front to rear) Creamy Celery-Zucchini Soup, chilly Gazpacho, and Vegetable Soup with Green Noodles. (See Index for recipe pages.)

HOT SOUPS

Summer Vegetable-Chicken Soup

This light soup is pictured on page 10. If desired, slice the broccoli while the chicken cooks—

  8 ounces broccoli
  1 whole chicken breast,
    split
  ¾ cup water
  1 medium onion, chopped
    (½ cup)
  1 stalk celery, thinly
    sliced (½ cup)
  3 cups chicken broth
    (see tip, page 87)
  1 teaspoon lemon juice
  ¼ teaspoon dried thyme,
    crushed
  ⅛ teaspoon pepper
  3 small tomatoes, peeled and
    cut into thin wedges

Remove the broccoli buds; thinly slice stalks (you should have a total of 2 cups buds and stalks). Set aside. In medium saucepan combine chicken, water, onion, and celery. Bring to boiling. Reduce heat; cover and simmer for 15 to 20 minutes or till chicken is tender. Remove chicken; cool slightly. Discard skin and bones; cut meat into short strips. Return chicken to cooking liquid.

Stir broccoli buds and stalks, chicken broth, lemon juice, thyme, and pepper into cooking liquid. Bring to boiling. Reduce heat; cover and simmer for 3 minutes. Add tomatoes; simmer, covered, about 4 minutes or till broccoli is crisp-tender and tomatoes are heated through. Season to taste with salt and pepper. Makes 4 to 6 servings.

Microwave cooking directions: Remove the broccoli buds; thinly slice stalks. In 2-quart nonmetal casserole combine chicken, water, onion, celery, and broccoli buds and stalks. Cook, covered with waxed paper, in countertop microwave oven on high power about 12 minutes or till chicken is tender. Remove chicken; cool slightly. Discard skin and bones; cut meat into short strips. Return chicken to casserole.

Stir in chicken broth, lemon juice, thyme, and pepper. Micro-cook, covered, for 3 to 4 minutes. Add tomatoes. Micro-cook, uncovered, about 45 seconds or till broccoli is crisp-tender and tomatoes are heated through. Season to taste.

Pea-Cottage Cheese Soup

  1 medium potato, chopped
    (1 cup)
  2 stalks celery, chopped
    (1 cup)
  1 medium onion, chopped
    (½ cup)
  ½ cup chicken broth
    (see tip, page 87)
  ½ teaspoon dried basil,
    crushed
  ¼ teaspoon salt
  ⅛ teaspoon pepper
  2 cups cream-style cottage
    cheese
  1 8-ounce can peas, drained
  1 cup milk

In 2-quart saucepan combine potato, celery, onion, chicken broth, basil, salt, and pepper. Bring to boiling. Reduce heat; cover and simmer for 15 minutes or till vegetables are tender.

Meanwhile, in blender container combine cottage cheese, peas, and milk; cover and blend till smooth. Stir into vegetables in saucepan; heat through. Makes 6 servings.

Chickumber Chowder

An attractive soup with elegant flavor pictured on page 18—

  1 medium onion, chopped
    (½ cup)
  ¼ cup butter *or* margarine
  ¼ cup all-purpose flour
  ½ teaspoon seasoned salt
  ¼ teaspoon white pepper
  3 cups chicken broth
    (see tip, page 87)
  5 medium cucumbers (about
    2½ pounds), peeled,
    halved lengthwise,
    seeded, and cut up
      • • •
  2 cups cubed cooked chicken
    or turkey (12 ounces)
  ½ cup long grain rice
  2 tablespoons lemon juice
  2 bay leaves
      • • •
  1 cup light cream
  ¼ cup snipped parsley

In 3-quart saucepan cook onion in butter or margarine till tender but not brown. Blend in flour, seasoned salt, and white pepper. Stir in chicken broth. Cook and stir till thickened and bubbly. Add cucumber. Cover and simmer for 10 minutes. Pour *half* the mixture at a time into blender container. Cover and blend on medium speed for 30 seconds. Return all to saucepan.

Stir in chicken or turkey, uncooked rice, lemon juice, and bay leaves. Return to boiling. Reduce heat; cover and simmer 20 to 25 minutes or till rice is tender. Remove bay leaves. Stir in cream and parsley; heat through. Season to taste with salt and pepper. Garnish with snipped parsley, if desired. Makes 6 servings.

Chinese Squash Soup

If you can't find Chinese squash at your supermarket or Oriental food store, substitute chayote, Chinese melon, or vegetable marrow —

¼ cup chopped onion
½ teaspoon curry powder
2 tablespoons cooking oil
2 tablespoons all-purpose
   flour
4 cups chicken broth
   (see tip, page 87)
2 tomatoes, peeled and
   chopped
1 apple, peeled and chopped
½ cup chopped carrot
¼ cup chopped green pepper
2 tablespoons snipped
   parsley
1 tablespoon lemon juice
1 teaspoon sugar
¼ teaspoon salt
   Dash pepper
1 Chinese squash, peeled and
   chopped (1½ cups)
1 cup diced cooked chicken

In 3-quart saucepan cook chopped onion and curry powder in hot oil till onion is tender but not brown. Blend in the flour. Stir in chicken broth, chopped tomatoes, apple, carrot, green pepper, parsley, lemon juice, sugar, salt, and pepper. Bring mixture to boiling, stirring occasionally. Reduce heat; cover and simmer for 15 minutes. Stir in Chinese squash and cooked chicken; simmer 15 minutes more or till squash is tender. Makes 6 to 8 servings.

Turkey Soup with Danish Dumplings

A good use for turkey bones that have some meat left on them —

1 meaty turkey carcass
8 cups water
1 tablespoon instant chicken
   bouillon granules
   ● ● ●
1 16-ounce can tomatoes,
   cut up
2 stalks celery, sliced
   (1 cup)
1 medium turnip, peeled
   and diced (1 cup)
1 medium carrot, sliced
   (½ cup)
1 medium onion, chopped
   (½ cup)
¼ cup snipped parsley
1 to 2 teaspoons salt
1 bay leaf
   Danish Dumplings
   (see recipe, page 90)

Cut up the turkey carcass to fit into a large Dutch oven. In the Dutch oven combine the carcass, water, and chicken bouillon granules. Bring to boiling. Reduce heat; cover and simmer for 1½ hours. Remove turkey carcass.

When carcass is cool enough to handle, remove meat from bones; discard bones. Return meat to cooking liquid along with *undrained* tomatoes, celery, turnip, carrot, onion, parsley, salt, and bay leaf. Bring to boiling. Reduce heat; cover and simmer 30 minutes or till vegetables are nearly tender. Remove bay leaf.

Drop Danish Dumpling dough from a tablespoon to make 12 mounds atop bubbling soup. Cover and simmer 20 minutes (do not lift cover). Makes 6 servings.

Pumpkin Soup

This pureed vegetable soup is shown on page 36 —

1 pound meaty beef short
   ribs
4 cups water
   ● ● ●
8 ounces pumpkin *or* winter
   squash, peeled, cubed,
   and cut up (about 3 cups)
1 medium potato, peeled and
   quartered
1 large carrot, quartered
1 medium onion, quartered
1½ teaspoons salt
¼ teaspoon white pepper
   ● ● ●
½ cup light cream (optional)

In 4-quart Dutch oven or large saucepan brown short ribs over low heat (add some cooking oil, if needed). Add water. Bring to boiling. Reduce heat; cover and simmer 1 hour. Remove ribs from broth. When ribs are cool enough to handle, cut meat from bones and return meat to broth; discard bones.

Add pumpkin or squash, potato, carrot, onion, salt, and white pepper to broth. Cover and simmer over medium heat for 45 minutes.

Pour *half* the mixture into blender container (or *one-third* of the mixture into food processor); cover and blend till smooth. Return blended mixture to saucepan. Repeat with remaining mixture. Heat through. Pour soup into individual soup bowls. Top each serving with a little cream, if desired. Do not stir before serving. Makes 6 servings.

Hot *SUMMER VEGETABLE-CHICKEN SOUP (left)* shows off fresh vegetables and chicken in a delightful broth. See recipe on page 8.

Sour-creamy *GREEN BEAN CHOWDER (center rear)* is welcome as an appetizer or for lunch. See recipe on page 16.

Prepare elegant *OYSTER-SPINACH SOUP (center front)* when unexpected guests arrive —it's ready in minutes. See recipe on page 22.

A delicate combination of vegetables and seasonings turns plain tomato soup into *HERBED TOMATO - VEGETABLE SOUP (right)*. See recipe on page 13.

Creamy Potato Soup

A potato soup with pieces of carrot and celery and the tang of dairy sour cream—

- 4 slices bacon, cut up
- 3 medium potatoes, peeled and chopped (3 cups)
- 1 large onion, chopped (1 cup)
- 1 medium carrot, chopped (½ cup)
- 1 stalk celery, chopped (½ cup)

• • •

- 4 cups milk
- 2 teaspoons salt
- ¼ teaspoon pepper

• • •

- 1 cup dairy sour cream
- 2 tablespoons all-purpose flour
- 2 teaspoons paprika

In large saucepan cook bacon till crisp. Drain bacon, reserving 3 table-spoons drippings in pan. Set bacon aside. Add chopped potatoes, onion, carrot, and celery to bacon drippings. Cover and cook over low heat about 20 minutes or till potatoes are tender, stirring occasionally. Stir in the milk, salt, and pepper; bring mixture to boiling.

Stir together sour cream, flour, and paprika; gradually stir about *1 cup* of the hot mixture into sour cream mixture. Return to remaining hot mixture in saucepan. Cook and stir just till mixture bubbles. Top with the bacon pieces. Serve immediately. Makes 6 to 8 servings.

Squash and Pea Soup

- 1 cup dry split peas
- 3 slices bacon, cut up
- 1 cup chopped onion
- 1 cup chopped green pepper
- 1 teaspoon instant chicken bouillon granules
- 1 12-ounce package frozen mashed squash
- 1 cup light cream

Rinse peas; set aside. In large sauce-pan cook bacon till crisp; drain, re-serving drippings in pan. Set bacon aside. Cook onion and green pepper in drippings just till tender; add peas, bouillon granules, 4 cups *water*, ¾ teaspoon *salt*, and ⅛ teaspoon *pepper*. Bring to boiling. Reduce heat; cover and simmer 1½ hours. Stir in frozen squash; cover and simmer 20 minutes or till heated through. Stir in cream and bacon; heat through. Makes 4 servings.

Easy Vegetable Soup

- 4 cups beef broth (see tip, page 87)
- 1 16-ounce can garbanzo beans, drained
- 1 16-ounce can tomatoes, cut up
- 1 8-ounce can cut green beans, drained
- ½ cup shell macaroni
- ½ cup chopped onion
- ½ cup finely chopped carrot
- ½ teaspoon dried basil, crushed
- ¼ teaspoon dried rosemary, crushed
- ¼ teaspoon dried thyme, crushed

In 4-quart Dutch oven combine all ingredients. Cover and simmer 30 to 40 minutes or till vegetables are ten-der. Makes 8 servings.

Buttermilk-Corn Chowder

- 2 slices bacon, cut up
- 1 small onion, chopped (¼ cup)
- 2 medium potatoes, peeled and cubed (2 cups)
- 2 cups fresh whole kernel corn *or* 1 10-ounce package frozen whole kernel corn
- 2 cups chicken broth (see tip, page 87)
- 1 stalk celery, chopped (½ cup)
- ½ teaspoon salt
- ¼ teaspoon pepper

• • •

- 2 tablespoons all-purpose flour
- 2 cups buttermilk
  Paprika *or* snipped parsley (optional)

In a 3-quart saucepan cook bacon till crisp. Drain bacon, reserving drip-pings in pan. Set bacon aside. Cook the chopped onion in bacon drip-pings till tender but not brown. Add the potatoes, corn, *1½ cups* of the chicken broth, the celery, salt, and pepper. Bring to boiling. Reduce heat; cover and simmer for 15 to 20 minutes or till vegetables are tender.

Combine flour and remaining ½ cup chicken broth; add to vegetable mixture. Cook and stir till thickened and bubbly. Reduce heat to low. Stir in buttermilk; heat through but *do not boil.* Top each serving with some of the bacon. Garnish with paprika or snipped parsley, if desired. Serve immediately. Makes 6 servings.

Chinese Hot Sour Soup

Make green onion fans by slicing the onion tops lengthwise, taking care to leave greens attached at the top of the onion bulb. Chill in a bowl of ice water until the tops curl—

4 ounces lean boneless pork
1 tablespoon cooking oil
4 cups chicken broth
    (see tip, page 87)
1 8-ounce can bamboo shoots, drained
1 3-ounce can sliced mushrooms, drained
2 tablespoons vinegar
1 tablespoon soy sauce
¼ teaspoon salt
¼ teaspoon white pepper *or* pepper
1 tablespoon cornstarch
2 tablespoons cold water
1 well-beaten egg
    Green onion fans

Partially freeze meat for easier slicing. Slice pork thinly into bite-size pieces. In 3-quart saucepan cook pork pieces in hot oil till lightly browned. Drain and set aside.

In same saucepan bring chicken broth to boiling. Add pork, bamboo shoots, and mushrooms. Simmer 5 minutes. Add vinegar, soy sauce, salt, and pepper. Blend together the cornstarch and water; stir into soup. Cook and stir till slightly thickened and bubbly. Stir broth to swirl; pour the beaten egg into center of swirl. Cook and stir 1 to 2 minutes more. Garnish each serving with a green onion fan. Makes 5 servings.

Herbed Tomato-Vegetable Soup

Prepare this soup, pictured on page 10, with either canned or fresh tomatoes—

1 medium onion, chopped
    (½ cup)
2 tablespoons butter *or* margarine
• • •
4 cups water
1 28-ounce can tomatoes, cut up *or* 2½ pounds fresh tomatoes, peeled and chopped (4 cups)
2 medium carrots, thinly sliced (1 cup)
2 stalks celery, chopped
    (1 cup)
1 tablespoon instant chicken bouillon granules
1 teaspoon sugar
1 teaspoon dried basil, crushed
½ teaspoon salt
½ teaspoon dried thyme, crushed
¼ teaspoon dried savory, crushed
⅛ teaspoon ground mace
⅛ teaspoon pepper
    Few dashes bottled hot pepper sauce

In large saucepan cook onion in butter or margarine till tender but not brown. Stir in water, *undrained* tomatoes, carrots, celery, bouillon granules, sugar, basil, salt, thyme, savory, mace, pepper, and hot pepper sauce. Bring to boiling. Reduce heat; cover and simmer about 40 minutes or till vegetables are tender. Makes 8 servings.

Vegetable Soup with Green Noodles

A dill-flavored soup that's shown on page 7—

1 medium rutabaga, diced
    (4 cups)
2 large onions, chopped
    (2 cups)
2 stalks celery, sliced
    (1 cup)
2 medium carrots, sliced
    (1 cup)
1 medium green pepper, chopped (½ cup)
1 clove garlic, minced
¼ cup butter *or* margarine
• • •
5 cups water
1 16-ounce can tomatoes, cut up
1 tablespoon snipped parsley
1 tablespoon salt
1 teaspoon sugar
½ teaspoon dried dillweed
¼ teaspoon pepper
    Green Noodles (see recipe, page 89)

In 5-quart Dutch oven combine the rutabaga, onions, celery, carrots, green pepper, garlic, and butter or margarine. Cover and cook about 10 minutes or till onion is tender but not brown, stirring occasionally.

Stir in the water, *undrained* tomatoes, parsley, salt, sugar, dried dillweed, and pepper. Bring to boiling. Reduce heat; cover and simmer 40 minutes. Stir in Green Noodles; cook, uncovered, for 10 to 12 minutes or till noodles are tender. Makes 8 to 10 servings.

·➤➤ HOT SOUPS ✄←·

Wonton Soup

1 beaten egg
¼ cup finely chopped onion
¼ cup finely chopped water chestnuts
1 tablespoon soy sauce
2 teaspoons grated fresh gingerroot
½ teaspoon sugar
¼ teaspoon salt
⅛ teaspoon pepper
½ pound ground pork
1 4½-ounce can shrimp, drained, deveined, and chopped
40 wonton skins or 10 egg roll skins, cut into quarters
8 cups water

• • •

6 cups chicken broth (see tip, page 87)
1 cup coarsely shredded Chinese cabbage
1 cup thinly sliced fresh mushrooms
1 6-ounce package frozen pea pods, thawed and halved lengthwise
½ cup thinly sliced bamboo shoots
4 green onions, bias-sliced into 1½-inch lengths

For filling, in bowl combine egg, onion, water chestnuts, soy sauce, gingerroot, sugar, salt, and pepper. Add ground pork and chopped shrimp; mix well.

Position wonton skin with one point toward you (refer to tip on page 41). Spoon 1 rounded teaspoon of filling just below center of skin. Fold bottom point of wonton skin over the filling; tuck point under filling. Roll up skin and filling, leaving about 1 inch at the top of skin. Moisten the right-hand corner of skin with water. Grasp the two lower corners of triangle; bring these corners toward you

below the filling. Overlap the left-hand corner over the right-hand corner; press to seal. Use 20 for soup; wrap, label, and freeze remaining 20 filled wontons.

In a large saucepan bring 8 cups water to boiling. Drop the wontons, one at a time, into boiling water. Simmer, uncovered, about 3 minutes. Remove from heat and rinse with cold water; drain well.

In same large saucepan bring chicken broth to boiling. Add Chinese cabbage, mushrooms, pea pods, bamboo shoots, and the precooked wontons. Simmer, uncovered, 4 to 5 minutes. Stir in green onion. Ladle soup into individual serving bowls. Makes 6 to 8 servings.

Creole Tomato Soup

¼ cup sliced green onion
1 clove garlic, minced
1 tablespoon butter or margarine
2 12-ounce cans (3 cups) vegetable juice cocktail
1 cup water
¼ cup long grain rice
1 teaspoon sugar
½ teaspoon salt
¼ teaspoon dried thyme, crushed
1 bay leaf
1 4½-ounce can shrimp, drained and deveined

In saucepan cook onion and garlic in butter or margarine till tender but not brown. Add vegetable juice cocktail, water, uncooked rice, sugar, salt, thyme, and bay leaf. Bring to boiling. Reduce heat; cover and simmer about 25 minutes or till rice is tender. Stir in shrimp. Heat through. Remove bay leaf before serving. Makes 4 servings.

Shrimp-Vegetable Broth

Float avocado slices atop servings of this soup, shown on page 18—

3 cups water
2 medium carrots, thinly sliced (1 cup)
4 teaspoons instant chicken bouillon granules

• • •

4 ounces frozen shelled shrimp (about 1 cup)
½ cup thinly sliced fresh mushrooms
½ cup frozen peas
4 green onions, bias-sliced into 1-inch pieces
1 small avocado, seeded, peeled, and sliced

In 1½-quart saucepan combine water, carrots, and bouillon granules. Bring to boiling. Reduce heat; cover and simmer for 25 to 30 minutes or till carrots are tender. Add shrimp, mushrooms, and peas. Simmer, uncovered, about 5 minutes or till shrimp and vegetables are tender. Stir in green onions. Ladle into individual serving bowls. Top each serving with avocado slices. Makes 6 to 8 servings.

Microwave cooking directions: Use ingredients as listed above. In 1½-quart nonmetal casserole combine water, carrots, and bouillon granules. Cook, covered, in countertop microwave oven on high power for 12 to 15 minutes or till carrots are tender. Add shrimp, mushrooms, and peas. Micro-cook, covered, for 4 to 5 minutes or till shrimp and vegetables are tender, stirring once. Stir in green onions. Serve as above.

Wonton Soup

14

Potato-Tomato Soup

This soup is shown on page 18—

4 cups cubed potatoes
3 medium tomatoes, peeled
  and chopped (2 cups)
1 cup chopped carrot
1 cup chopped celery
3 10½-ounce cans *condensed*
  beef broth
1 small bay leaf
2 slices pumpernickel bread
1 cup dairy sour cream

In large saucepan combine first 6 ingredients. Bring to boiling. Reduce heat; cover and simmer 20 minutes or till vegetables are tender.

Meanwhile, cube bread; place bread cubes on baking sheet. Toast in 350° oven 10 minutes; set aside. Remove bay leaf from soup. Top each serving with toast cubes and a dollop of sour cream. Makes 8 servings.

Cheese Soup

Pictured on page 18—

½ cup finely chopped carrot
½ cup finely chopped onion
¼ cup finely chopped celery
2 tablespoons butter
¼ cup all-purpose flour
1 cup chicken broth
  (see tip, page 87)
¼ teaspoon salt
2 cups light cream *or* milk
1½ cups shredded American
  cheese (6 ounces)

In covered saucepan cook carrot, onion, and celery in butter over low heat till tender. Stir in flour. Add broth and salt. Cook and stir till thickened and bubbly. Stir in cream or milk and cheese till cheese melts and soup is heated through. *Do not boil.* Makes 4 to 6 servings.

Creamy Borscht

After the egg yolk-sour cream mixture is added, be sure that the soup does not boil—

4 cups Browned Beef Stock
  (see recipe, page 85)
  or Vegetable Stock
  (see recipe, page 88)
4 medium beets, peeled
  and cubed (3 cups)
2 medium carrots, chopped
  (1 cup)
1 medium onion, chopped
  (½ cup)
1 bay leaf
1 tablespoon vinegar
1 teaspoon sugar
1 teaspoon salt
¼ teaspoon pepper
    ● ● ●
½ small head cabbage,
  shredded (3 cups)
1 16-ounce can tomatoes,
  cut up
2 slightly beaten egg yolks
½ cup dairy sour cream

In a 4-quart Dutch oven combine Browned Beef Stock or Vegetable Stock, beets, carrots, onion, bay leaf, vinegar, sugar, salt, and pepper. Bring to boiling. Reduce heat; cover and simmer for 40 minutes. Stir in cabbage and *undrained* tomatoes. Cover and cook 30 to 35 minutes more or till vegetables are tender. Remove bay leaf.

Blend egg yolks and sour cream; gradually stir in about *1 cup* of the hot mixture. Return to Dutch oven; heat through, stirring constantly over low heat. *Do not boil.* Serve immediately. Makes 6 to 8 servings.

Green Bean Chowder

Pictured on page 10—

1 9-ounce package frozen
  French-style green beans
1 cup chopped carrot
1 cup chopped potato
½ cup chopped green pepper
1 teaspoon dried savory,
  crushed
¼ teaspoon dried dillweed
1 cup dairy sour cream
1 tablespoon all-purpose
  flour
2 cups milk

Partially thaw beans; chop and set aside. In 3-quart saucepan mix carrot, potato, green pepper, savory, dillweed, 1 teaspoon *salt*, and ¼ teaspoon *pepper*. Stir in 2 cups *water*. Bring to boiling; reduce heat and simmer 10 minutes. Add beans; cook 5 minutes more or till *vegetables* are tender. Blend sour cream and flour; stir in about *1 cup* of the hot mixture. Return to saucepan. Stir in milk; heat till slightly thickened; *do not boil.* Makes 8 servings.

Matzo Ball Soup

4 cups chicken broth
  (see tip, page 87)
2 medium carrots, sliced
  Matzo Balls (see recipe,
  page 91)
2 tablespoons snipped
  parsley

In large saucepan bring broth to boiling. Add carrots. Reduce heat; simmer, uncovered, 10 minutes. Drop chilled Matzo Ball dough by rounded tablespoonfuls into simmering broth, making 8 balls. Cover; simmer 30 minutes. Do not lift lid. Sprinkle with parsley. Serves 8.

Swiss-Broccoli Soup

2 teaspoons instant chicken
    bouillon granules
1 10-ounce package frozen
    cut broccoli
2 cups milk
1 cup shredded process Swiss
    cheese (4 ounces)
⅛ teaspoon ground nutmeg
¼ cup all-purpose flour

In saucepan heat bouillon granules in
1½ cups *water* till dissolved. Add
broccoli; cover and cook for 8 to 10
minutes or till tender. Add milk,
cheese, nutmeg, and dash *pepper*.
Cook and stir till cheese melts. Combine flour and ½ cup cold *water*; stir
into broccoli mixture. Cook and stir
till thickened and bubbly. Makes 4 to
6 servings.

Mushroom-Barley Soup

8 ounces fresh mushrooms,
    sliced (3 cups)
1 medium green pepper,
    chopped (½ cup)
1 medium onion, chopped
    (½ cup)
1 clove garlic, minced
2 tablespoons butter *or*
    margarine
¾ cup quick-cooking barley
¾ teaspoon ground sage
½ teaspoon salt
5 cups beef broth
    (see tip, page 87)

In 3-quart covered saucepan cook
mushrooms, green pepper, onion,
and garlic in butter or margarine
about 5 minutes or till tender but not
brown. Stir in barley, sage, and salt.
Add broth; bring to boiling. Reduce
heat; cover and simmer 20 to 25
minutes or till barley is tender. Makes
6 servings.

Creamy Celery-Zucchini Soup

This soup is pictured on page 7—

3 cups sliced celery
3 green onions, finely
    chopped
2 tablespoons butter
1 medium zucchini
1 tablespoon instant chicken
    bouillon granules
1½ cups milk
1 tablespoon cornstarch
2 sprigs parsley, snipped

In 3-quart covered saucepan cook
celery and onions in butter for 5 to 10
minutes. Meanwhile, cut zucchini in
half lengthwise. Slice zucchini. Add
zucchini, bouillon granules, 1 cup *water,* and ¼ teaspoon *salt* to saucepan.
Cover; simmer 10 minutes. Blend
milk and cornstarch; add to saucepan. Cook and stir till thickened and
bubbly. Season to taste. Sprinkle
parsley atop each serving. Makes 4
servings.

Tomato Tune-Up

3 cups tomato juice
½ cup sliced celery
2 thin slices onion
4 whole cloves
1 bay leaf
2 dashes bottled hot pepper
    sauce
1 10½-ounce can *condensed*
    beef broth
⅓ cup dry white wine

In saucepan combine first 6 ingredients. Bring to boiling. Reduce heat;
cover and simmer 20 minutes. Strain
soup, discarding seasonings. Return
soup to saucepan; add condensed
broth and wine. Return to boiling.
Float a thin lemon slice in each bowl,
if desired. Makes 8 servings.

Celery-Spinach Soup

1 10¾-ounce can *condensed*
    chicken broth
1 10-ounce package frozen
    spinach
2 cups chopped celery
1 cup chopped onion
1 cup cream-style cottage
    cheese
2 cups milk
½ teaspoon salt
⅛ teaspoon pepper
½ cup dairy sour cream

In 3-quart saucepan combine condensed broth, frozen spinach, celery,
and onion. Bring to boiling. Reduce
heat; cover and simmer 10 minutes or
till vegetables are tender. Transfer to
blender container; add cottage
cheese. Cover and blend till smooth.
Return mixture to saucepan. Stir in
milk, salt, and pepper; heat through.
Top each serving with a dollop of sour
cream. Makes 6 servings.

Cheese-Spinach Soup

½ cup chopped onion
½ cup chopped celery
¼ cup butter *or* margarine
¼ cup all-purpose flour
½ teaspoon salt
⅛ teaspoon pepper
4 cups milk
1 10-ounce package frozen
    chopped spinach, thawed
1½ cups shredded American
    cheese (6 ounces)

In 3-quart saucepan cook onion and
celery in butter or margarine till onion
is tender. Stir in flour, salt, and pepper. Add milk all at once; cook and
stir till thickened and bubbly. Stir in
spinach and cheese; cook and stir till
cheese melts. Makes 4 to 6 servings.

Serve rich and creamy CHEESE SOUP (left) as a delicious accompaniment for a sandwich at lunchtime, or to start a meal with flair. See recipe on page 16.

Shrimp, carrots, mushrooms, peas, and green onions float in SHRIMP-VEGETABLE BROTH (front), an elegant appetizer soup. See recipe on page 14.

Cucumbers and lemon juice make CHICKUMBER CHOWDER (center rear) a chicken soup with sophistication. See recipe on page 8.

Pass pumpernickel croutons and sour cream to serve with hearty POTATO-TOMATO SOUP (right). It's already brimming with favorite vegetables. See recipe on page 16.

Butternut Squash and Apple Soup

This unusual soup uses bread crumbs as its thickener—

- 1 small butternut squash, halved and seeded (16 ounces)
- 3 medium green apples, peeled, cored, and coarsely chopped (3 cups)
- 2 10¾-ounce cans *condensed* chicken broth
- 1½ cups water
- 3 slices white bread, torn into pieces
- 1 medium onion, chopped (½ cup)
- 1 teaspoon salt
- ¼ teaspoon dried rosemary, crushed
- ¼ teaspoon dried marjoram, crushed
- ⅛ teaspoon freshly ground pepper
- ¼ cup whipping cream
  Snipped parsley

Peel and cut up squash. In 4-quart Dutch oven combine the squash, apples, condensed chicken broth, water, bread, onion, salt, rosemary, marjoram, and pepper. Bring to boiling. Reduce heat; simmer, uncovered, for 45 minutes. Turn *one-fourth* of the soup mixture into a blender container. Cover and blend till smooth; set aside. Repeat with remaining mixture, one-fourth at a time. Return all the soup to the Dutch oven. Bring to boiling. Reduce heat to simmering. Stir in cream. Garnish each serving with snipped parsley. Makes 6 to 8 servings.

Mexicali Bean Soup

- ½ cup chopped onion
- 1 clove garlic, minced
- 2 tablespoons cooking oil
- 2 16-ounce cans red kidney beans, drained
- 1 16-ounce can tomatoes, cut up
- 1 16-ounce can cream-style corn
- 1 4-ounce can green chili peppers, rinsed, seeded and chopped
- 1 tablespoon instant chicken bouillon granules
- 1 teaspoon ground cumin
  Puffy Cheese Noodles (see recipe, page 89)

In 5-quart Dutch oven cook onion and garlic in oil till onion is tender. Stir in next 6 ingredients, 6 cups *water,* 2 teaspoons *salt,* and ¼ teaspoon *pepper.* Cover and simmer 25 minutes. Add Puffy Cheese Noodles; simmer, uncovered, 10 to 12 minutes or till noodles are done. Serves 6 to 8.

Micro-Cooking

A countertop microwave oven saves time in preparing soups and stews. Use it for a single preparation step, such as melting butter, cooking onion in butter, or cooking bacon (see timings below). Or, use it to prepare entire recipes (see Index— Microwave Cooking).

For all recipes in this book, use the high-power setting of a countertop microwave oven. Use only nonmetal containers.

• Cook ½ cup chopped onion in 1 tablespoon butter, covered, 2 to 3 minutes; stir once.

• Cook 4 slices bacon between layers of paper toweling in a shallow dish, about 3 minutes.

Turn-About Gazpacho

Use a food processor if you like, but process only one-third of the vegetable mixture at a time—

- 1 16-ounce can tomatoes
- 1 10½-ounce can *condensed* beef broth
- 1 small cucumber, cut up
- 2 stalks celery, sliced (1 cup)
- ½ medium green pepper, cut up
- 4 sprigs parsley
- ¼ cup sliced green onion
- ¼ teaspoon garlic salt
- ¼ teaspoon freshly ground pepper
  Dash bottled hot pepper sauce
- 5 or 6 pats butter *or* margarine
- 1 cup plain *or* seasoned croutons

In blender container combine *half each* of the tomatoes, beef broth, and cucumber. Cover and blend till slightly chopped. Add *half each* of the celery, green pepper, and parsley. Blend just till vegetables are coarsely chopped; pour into a 2-quart saucepan. Repeat with remaining tomatoes, broth, cucumber, celery, green pepper, and parsley. (Or, coarsely chop vegetables by hand.) Stir in green onion, garlic salt, pepper, and bottled hot pepper sauce. Cover and simmer 18 to 20 minutes or till vegetables are barely tender. Top each serving with a pat of butter or margarine and sprinkle with croutons. Makes 5 or 6 servings.

CREAM OF FRESH VEGETABLE SOUP

1½ cups chicken broth
    (see tip, page 87)
½ cup chopped onion
    Desired vegetable and
    seasonings (see chart
    below)
2 tablespoons butter
2 tablespoons all-purpose
    flour
½ teaspoon salt
    Few dashes white pepper
1 cup milk

In saucepan combine chicken broth, chopped onion, and one of the vegetable-seasoning combinations from chart. (Or, substitute an equal amount of frozen vegetable, if desired.) Bring mixture to boiling. Reduce heat; cover and simmer the time indicated in the chart or till vegetable is tender. (Remove bay leaf if using broccoli.)

Place *half* the vegetable mixture into a blender container or food processor. Cover and blend 30 to 60 seconds or till smooth. Pour into bowl. Repeat with remaining vegetable mixture; set all aside.

In the same saucepan melt the butter. Blend in flour, salt, and pepper. Add the milk all at once. Cook and stir till mixture is thickened and bubbly. Stir in the blended vegetable mixture. Cook and stir till soup is heated through. Season to taste with additional salt and pepper. Serves 3 or 4.

Vegetable	Seasonings	Cooking Time	Yield
2 cups cut asparagus	1 teaspoon lemon juice ⅛ teaspoon ground mace	8 minutes	3½ cups
1½ cups cut green beans	½ teaspoon dried savory, crushed	20 to 30 minutes	3 cups
2 cups cut broccoli	½ teaspoon dried thyme, crushed 1 small bay leaf Dash garlic powder	10 minutes	3½ cups
1 cup sliced carrots	1 tablespoon snipped parsley ½ teaspoon dried basil, crushed	12 minutes	3½ cups
2 cups sliced cauliflower	½ to ¾ teaspoon curry powder	10 minutes	3½ cups
1½ cups chopped celery	2 tablespoons snipped parsley ½ teaspoon dried basil, crushed	15 minutes	3 cups
1 cup sliced fresh mushrooms	⅛ teaspoon ground nutmeg	5 minutes	2⅔ cups
1½ cups shelled peas	¼ cup shredded lettuce 2 tablespoons diced fully cooked ham ¼ teaspoon dried sage, crushed	8 minutes	3½ cups
1 cup sliced potatoes	½ teaspoon dried dillweed	10 minutes	3 cups
4 medium tomatoes, peeled, quartered, and seeded	¼ teaspoon dried basil, crushed	15 minutes	3⅓ cups
1½ cups cut unpeeled zucchini	Several dashes ground nutmeg	5 minutes	3⅓ cups

QUICK-SOUPS

HOT SOUPS

Oyster-Spinach Soup

Pictured on page 10—

2 cups milk
2 10¾-ounce cans condensed
   cream of chicken soup
2 9- *or* 10-ounce packages
   frozen chopped spinach in
   cream sauce
2 8-ounce cans oysters
1 cup dry white wine
¼ teaspoon white pepper

In saucepan or Dutch oven stir milk
into condensed soup. Remove
spinach from pouches; add to soup.
Cook and stir over medium heat,
breaking up spinach with a fork till
thawed; simmer, uncovered, 10
minutes, stirring occasionally. Stir in
undrained oysters, wine, and
pepper. Cook and stir till heated
through. Garnish with lemon slices,
if desired. Makes 8 servings.

Spaghetti-Corn Soup

1 envelope *regular* onion
   soup mix
2 15-ounce cans spaghetti
   rings with meatballs
   in tomato sauce
1 16-ounce can cream-style
   corn
   Grated parmesan cheese

Prepare onion soup mix according
to package directions. Stir in
spaghetti and meatballs and corn;
heat through. Serve with grated
parmesan. Makes 8 servings.

Caldo Con Queso

2½ cups water
2 canned green chili peppers,
   seeded and cut up
1 tomato, peeled and diced
½ teaspoon garlic salt
¼ teaspoon pepper
   ● ● ●
1 13-ounce can (1⅔ cups)
   evaporated milk
1 10¾-ounce can condensed
   cream of potato soup
1 10¾-ounce can condensed
   cream of onion soup
8 ounces monterey jack
   cheese

In 3-quart saucepan combine water,
green chili peppers, tomato, garlic
salt, and pepper. Bring to boiling.
Reduce heat; cover and simmer 5
minutes. Blend in evaporated milk,
condensed cream of potato soup,
and condensed cream of onion
soup. Heat through.
   Meanwhile, cut the monterey jack
cheese into small cubes; divide
cheese cubes evenly among soup
bowls. Ladle hot soup over cheese;
serve immediately. Makes 6 to 8
servings.

Sun's Up Soup

2 cups milk
1 10¾-ounce can condensed
   cream of potato soup
½ of a 3-ounce package sliced
   smoked beef, snipped
½ cup shredded American
   cheese (2 ounces)
1 slice bread, toasted and
   cut into triangles

In 2-quart saucepan gradually stir
milk into soup; add smoked beef
and cheese. Cook and stir about
5 minutes or till mixture is heated
through. Top each serving with a
toast triangle. Makes 4 servings.

Portuguese Ham and Egg Soup

1 10½-ounce can condensed
   chicken with rice soup
1 soup can water (1¼ cups)
¼ cup finely chopped fully
   cooked ham
2 green onions, thinly sliced
2 teaspoons lemon juice
1 beaten egg
   Ground nutmeg

In saucepan heat soup and water
according to label directions; add
ham, onions, and lemon juice. Stir
about *half* the hot mixture into
beaten egg; return to saucepan.
Heat and stir till mixture simmers.
Sprinkle lightly with nutmeg. Makes
4 servings.

Appetizer Broccoli Soup

2 10-ounce packages frozen chopped broccoli
2 10¾-ounce cans condensed cream of mushroom soup
2 soup cans milk (2½ cups)
½ cup dry white wine
¼ cup butter *or* margarine
½ teaspoon dried tarragon, crushed
Dash white pepper

In large saucepan cook broccoli according to package directions; drain. Add soup, milk, wine, butter or margarine, tarragon, and pepper. Heat through. Makes 8 servings.

Corn-Peanut Chowder

2 cups water
1 envelope *regular* chicken noodle soup mix
1 tablespoon finely chopped onion
¼ teaspoon salt
2 cups milk
1 16-ounce can cream-style corn
2 tablespoons creamy peanut butter

In 3-quart saucepan bring water to boiling; add soup mix, onion, and salt. Reduce heat; cover and simmer about 10 minutes or till noodles are tender. Stir in milk, corn, and peanut butter; heat through. Serves 4 to 6.

Shortcut Minestrone

4 slices bacon, cut up
1 envelope *regular* tomato-vegetable soup mix
4 cups water
1 16-ounce can red kidney beans, drained
1 10-ounce package frozen mixed vegetables
Grated parmesan cheese

In 3-quart saucepan cook bacon till crisp; drain and set aside. In same saucepan blend together dry soup mix, water, beans, and mixed vegetables. Bring to boiling. Reduce heat; cover and simmer 10 to 15 minutes. Pass the cooked bacon and grated parmesan to sprinkle atop. Makes 5 or 6 servings.

Serving Dishes

When choosing serving dishes, consider the soup you're preparing. Chunky soups are attractive in shallow or deep soup bowls: Knife-and-fork soups and stews require shallow soup plates. Drink soups without solid pieces from mugs or cups, if you like. And for lunches away from home, don't forget wide-mouthed vacuum containers to keep soup hot.

In the kitchen, ladle soup right from the kettle. Or, serve it at the table from a tureen or casserole.

Salami-Bean Chowder

2 cups water
2 stalks celery, chopped (1 cup)
4 ounces salami, cut into small chunks (about ¾ cup)
1 medium onion, chopped (½ cup)
1 16-ounce can pork and beans in tomato sauce
1 10¾-ounce can condensed tomato soup
1 teaspoon worcestershire sauce

In medium saucepan combine water, celery, salami, and onion; bring to boiling. Reduce heat; cover and simmer 15 minutes. Stir in remaining ingredients; heat through. Makes 6 servings.

Egg-Lemon Soup

1 envelope *regular* chicken noodle soup mix
2 tablespoons cold water
1 tablespoon cornstarch
2 eggs
2 tablespoons lemon juice

Prepare soup mix according to package directions. Blend water and cornstarch; stir into soup. Cook and stir till bubbly. In small mixer bowl beat eggs about 4 minutes or till light. Gradually stir in *1 cup* of the hot soup. Return all to saucepan. Stir in lemon juice. Cook, stirring constantly, 2 minutes. Serves 8.

COLD SOUPS

Gazpacho

An uncooked, cold soup that's pictured on page 7—

4 large tomatoes
1 small cucumber, chopped (1 cup)
1 medium green pepper, chopped (½ cup)
1 stalk celery, chopped (½ cup)
1 small onion, finely chopped (¼ cup)
1 clove garlic, minced
1 13¾-ounce can chicken broth
2 tablespoons lemon juice
1 tablespoon cooking oil
1 teaspoon sugar
1 teaspoon salt
¼ teaspoon pepper
   Dash bottled hot pepper sauce
   Croutons

Plunge tomatoes into boiling water for 30 seconds to loosen skins; then immerse in cold water. Slip skins off. Coarsely chop tomatoes (you should have about 2½ cups).

In large bowl combine chopped tomatoes, cucumber, green pepper, celery, onion, and garlic. Stir in chicken broth, lemon juice, oil, sugar, salt, pepper, and hot pepper sauce. Cover; chill thoroughly. Garnish each serving with croutons. Serves 8 to 10.

Note: For a smoother soup, combine all ingredients *except* croutons as directed above. Place *half* the mixture at a time in blender container (or *one-third* of the mixture at a time in a food processor). Cover and blend till smooth. Chill and serve as above.

Buttermilk-Shrimp Bisque

1 teaspoon onion salt
2 teaspoons prepared mustard
½ teaspoon sugar
½ teaspoon dried dillweed
   Dash bottled hot pepper sauce
4 cups buttermilk
1 4½-ounce can small shrimp, drained and deveined
1 small cucumber, chopped (1 cup)
½ cup chopped green pepper
½ cup chopped celery
1 2-ounce jar diced pimiento, drained (¼ cup)

In 1½-quart bowl mix onion salt, mustard, sugar, dillweed, and hot pepper sauce. Stir in buttermilk, shrimp, cucumber, green pepper, celery, and pimiento. Cover; chill. Makes 8 to 10 servings.

Zucchini-Tomato Soup

½ cup chopped onion
½ cup chopped green pepper
¼ cup water
1 18-ounce can (2¼ cups) tomato juice
2 medium zucchini, quartered lengthwise and sliced (2 cups)
1 8-ounce can whole kernel corn, drained
¼ teaspoon salt
2 cups buttermilk

In 2-quart saucepan cook onion and green pepper in water, covered, about 5 minutes or till vegetables are tender. Add tomato juice, zucchini, corn, and salt. Simmer, covered, 30 minutes. Cool. Stir into buttermilk. Cover; chill. Makes 8 to 10 servings.

Golden Squash and Carrot Bisque

3 medium yellow summer squash, sliced (3 cups)
2 medium carrots, sliced (1 cup)
1 medium onion, chopped (½ cup)
1 13¾-ounce can chicken broth
½ teaspoon salt
1 13-ounce can (1⅔ cups) evaporated milk
   Snipped parsley

In 2-quart saucepan combine sliced summer squash, carrots, onion, chicken broth, and salt. Bring to boiling. Reduce heat; cover and simmer for 15 to 20 minutes or till carrots are just tender. Turn *half* the mixture into blender container or food processor; cover and blend till smooth. Pour into bowl; repeat with remaining mixture. Stir in evaporated milk. Cover and chill. Sprinkle with snipped parsley. Makes 6 servings.

Microwave cooking directions: Use ingredients as listed above. In 2-quart nonmetal casserole combine squash, carrots, and onion; sprinkle with salt. Cook, covered with waxed paper, in countertop microwave oven on high power about 15 minutes or till vegetables are tender, stirring once.

In blender container or food processor combine *half* the cooked vegetables and *half* the chicken broth; cover and blend till mixture is smooth. Turn into a bowl. Repeat with remaining vegetables and broth. Stir in the evaporated milk. Cover and chill. Sprinkle with parsley.

Buttermilk-Shrimp Bisque
Chilled Beet Soup
(see recipe, page 30)

Vichyssoise

Make this elegant first-course soup ahead of time using either chicken broth or White Stock—

2 leeks
1 small onion, sliced
2 tablespoons butter *or* margarine
• • •
3 small potatoes, peeled and sliced (2½ cups)
2 cups chicken broth (see tip, page 87) *or* White Stock (see recipe, page 88)
1 teaspoon salt
1½ cups milk
1 cup whipping cream
Snipped chives

Remove tops from leeks; slice leeks (you should have about ⅔ cup). In 2-quart saucepan cook leeks and onion in butter or margarine till vegetables are tender but not brown. Stir in sliced potatoes, chicken broth or White Stock, and salt. Bring to boiling. Reduce heat; cover and simmer for 35 to 40 minutes or till potatoes are very tender.

Place *half* of the mixture in blender container or food processor; cover and blend till mixture is smooth. Pour into bowl. Repeat with remaining mixture. Return all mixture to saucepan; stir in milk. Season to taste with additional salt and white pepper. Bring to boiling, stirring frequently. Cool. Stir in whipping cream. Cover and chill thoroughly before serving. Garnish with snipped chives. Makes 4 to 6 servings.

Creamy Green Pepper Soup

1 medium green pepper chopped (½ cup)
1 small onion, chopped (¼ cup)
¼ cup water
1 10¾-ounce can condensed cream of celery soup
1¾ cups milk

In 1½-quart covered saucepan cook green pepper and onion in water, till tender. Do not drain. Stir in condensed soup, then the milk. Heat through, stirring occasionally. Cover and chill thoroughly. Float green pepper rings atop, if desired. Makes 3 or 4 servings.

Curried Coconut Soup

1 small onion, chopped (¼ cup)
1 teaspoon curry powder
¼ cup water
3 cups milk
1 cup flaked coconut
2 whole cloves
½ teaspoon salt
2 beaten egg yolks
Toasted coconut (optional)

In a 2-quart saucepan cook onion and curry powder in water till onion is tender. Stir in milk, coconut, cloves, and salt. Simmer, covered, for 15 minutes. Strain mixture through a sieve. Stir about *1 cup* of the hot milk mixture into the egg yolks. Return to remaining milk mixture in saucepan. Cook and stir about 2 minutes or till mixture thickens slightly. Remove from heat; cover and chill. Garnish each serving with toasted coconut, if desired. Makes 4 to 6 servings.

Crab-Avocado Soup

This sophisticated soup is made smooth with a blender or a food processor. Remember it for a special occasion—

1 large apple, peeled and chopped (1 cup)
1 stalk celery, finely chopped (½ cup)
1 tablespoon butter *or* margarine
1 tablespoon all-purpose flour
2 cups chicken broth (see tip, page 87)
• • •
1 medium avocado, seeded, peeled, and cut up
1 7½-ounce can crab meat, drained, flaked, and cartilage removed
½ cup light cream
Salt
Pepper
Snipped chives

In medium saucepan cook apple and celery in butter or margarine about 5 minutes or till apple and celery are tender. Stir in the flour. Add chicken broth all at once; cook and stir till mixture is thickened and bubbly.

Place *half* the mixture in blender container or food processor. Add *half* the avocado. Cover and blend till smooth. Pour into bowl. Repeat with remaining broth mixture and avocado. Stir in the crab meat and light cream. Season to taste with some salt and pepper. Cover and chill. Before serving, garnish each serving with snipped chives. Makes 6 to 8 servings.

Blender Broccoli Soup

½ cup water
2 teaspoons instant beef
    bouillon granules
1 10-ounce package frozen
    chopped broccoli
1 cup milk
1 cup light cream
¼ teaspoon onion salt
    Dash pepper
    Dash ground nutmeg

In saucepan heat water and bouillon granules to boiling; add broccoli. Cover and simmer mixture for 3 minutes. Do not drain.

In blender container or food processor combine *half* the broccoli mixture and *half* the milk. Cover and blend till broccoli is very fine. Add *half* the cream, the onion salt, pepper, and nutmeg. Cover and blend about 1 minute or till smooth. Set mixture aside. Repeat with remaining broccoli, milk, and cream. Cover and chill. Stir before serving. If desired, garnish with sour cream and snipped chives. Makes 6 to 8 servings.

Serving Ideas for Cold Soups

Though traditionally thought of as appetizers, cold soups make tasty alternatives for refreshing snacks. They're great with a salad or sandwich for a summer lunch. And sweet fruit soups make delightful desserts or brunch fare.

Be sure to serve cold soups very cold in chilled mugs, cups, sherbet dishes, or bowls. Or, surround serving bowls with crushed ice in glass icers.

Since cold soups are usually not a main dish, offer ½- to ¼-cup servings.

Jellied Consommé

If using homemade beef broth, be sure that you clarify the broth before preparing this recipe—

4 cups beef broth (see
    tip, page 87) *or* 2
    tablespoons instant
    beef bouillon granules
    dissolved in 4 cups hot
    water
1 small onion, chopped
    (¼ cup)
½ of a medium green pepper,
    chopped (¼ cup)
1 tablespoon snipped parsley
1 teaspoon worcestershire
    sauce
    • • •
2 tablespoons dry sherry
2 tablespoons water
1 envelope unflavored
    gelatin
½ cup whipping cream
    (optional)
¼ teaspoon curry powder
    (optional)

In saucepan combine beef broth, onion, green pepper, parsley, and worcestershire sauce. Bring to boiling. Reduce heat; simmer, uncovered, for 15 minutes to reduce liquid slightly (it should measure 3 to 3½ cups). Strain mixture, discarding vegetables. Return the strained broth to saucepan.

In small bowl combine sherry and water; sprinkle gelatin over liquid and let stand to soften gelatin. Stir gelatin mixture into broth; heat and stir till gelatin dissolves. Pour into a large bowl. Chill till set.

Before serving, whip cream and curry powder just to stiff peaks. Break up consommé with a fork; spoon into serving dishes. Top each serving with a dollop of the whipped cream. Makes 4 to 6 servings.

Asparagus Soup

¾ pound asparagus, cut up
    or 1 10-ounce package
    frozen cut asparagus
1 thin slice onion
½ cup boiling water
1 cup milk
½ cup light cream

In covered saucepan cook asparagus and onion slice in water 8 to 10 minutes or till crisp-tender; do not drain. Cool slightly. In blender container or food processor combine the undrained asparagus and onion, milk, cream, ½ teaspoon *salt*, and dash *pepper*. Cover and blend till smooth. Chill for 3 to 4 hours. Stir or blend before serving. Makes 4 to 6 servings.

Berry-Buttermilk Soup

2 cups fresh *or* frozen
    loose-pack blueberries
    or strawberries,
1½ cups water
½ cup sugar
½ teaspoon finely shredded
    orange peel
2 tablespoons orange juice
2 cups buttermilk

Thaw berries, if frozen; drain. If desired, set aside 5 or 6 berries for garnish. In 1½-quart saucepan combine berries, water, sugar, orange peel, and juice. Bring to boiling. Reduce heat; cover and simmer 20 minutes. Cool 30 minutes.

Pour into blender container; cover and blend till smooth. Stir in the buttermilk. Cover and chill thoroughly. If desired, garnish each serving with a reserved berry or a thin orange slice. Makes 5 or 6 servings.

COLD SOUPS

Cucumber-Cream Soup

3 medium cucumbers, peeled,
    seeded, and chopped
    (3 cups)
1 small onion, chopped
    (¼ cup)
3 tablespoons butter *or*
    margarine
¼ cup all-purpose flour
3 cups chicken broth
    (see tip, page 87)
1 cup whipping cream

In 2-quart saucepan cook cucumbers
and onion, covered, in butter or margarine about 15 minutes or till tender.
Stir in flour. Add chicken broth and
whipping cream; cook and stir till
thickened and bubbly. Pour *half* the
mixture into blender container or
food processor. Cover and blend till
mixture is smooth. Set aside. Repeat
with remaining mixture. Cover and
chill. Garnish with additional
cucumber slices, if desired. Makes 10
to 12 servings.
   Microwave cooking directions: Use
ingredients as listed above. In a
2-quart nonmetal bowl or casserole
place cucumbers, onion, and butter
or margarine. Cover with waxed
paper and cook in a countertop
microwave oven on high power
about 7 minutes or till onion is tender.
Stir in flour. Add chicken broth and
cream. Cover and micro-cook 8 minutes or till thickened and bubbly, stirring every 2 minutes. Blend *half* the
mixture in blender container or food
processor till smooth. Set aside; repeat with remaining. Cover and chill.
Serve as directed above.

Chilled Pea Soup
Creamy Fruit Soup

Apple-Raisin Soup

2 cups apple juice *or* cider
2 large cooking apples,
    peeled and cubed (2 cups)
¼ cup light raisins
2 inches stick cinnamon
1 tablespoon brown sugar
1 tablespoon brandy

In 2-quart saucepan combine first 4
ingredients. Cover; simmer 15 minutes or till apples are tender. Stir in
sugar and brandy. Cover; chill. Remove stick cinnamon before serving.
Makes 3 or 4 servings.

Creamy Fruit Soup

1 10-ounce package frozen
    raspberries, blueberries,
    strawberries, peaches,
    or mixed fruit, thawed
1 cup water
¼ cup sugar
2 inches stick cinnamon
    Dash ground nutmeg
    Dash ground cloves
1 tablespoon water
1 tablespoon cornstarch
2 tablespoons lemon juice
1 cup dairy sour cream
½ cup milk

Drain fruit, reserving syrup (cut up
large pieces of fruit). In 1½-quart
saucepan combine reserved syrup,
the 1 cup water, sugar, cinnamon,
nutmeg, and cloves. Bring to boiling;
reduce heat and simmer, uncovered,
for 5 minutes. Remove stick cinnamon. Blend the 1 tablespoon water
and cornstarch; stir into saucepan.
Cook and stir till thickened and bubbly. Remove from heat. Add lemon
juice. Cool to room temperature.
Blend in sour cream and fruit. Stir in
milk. Cover and chill. Garnish with
strips of lemon peel, if desired. Makes
4 to 6 servings.

Chilled Pea Soup

2 cups fresh *or* 1 10-ounce
    package frozen peas
2 cups shredded lettuce
1 13¾-ounce can chicken
    broth
⅓ cup water
¼ cup tomato juice
¼ cup finely chopped green
    onion
1 tablespoon snipped parsley
½ teaspoon salt
¼ teaspoon white pepper
¼ teaspoon dried thyme,
    crushed
½ cup whipping cream

In 2-quart saucepan combine peas,
lettuce, chicken broth, water, tomato
juice, onion, parsley, salt, white pepper, and thyme. Bring to boiling. Reduce heat; cover and simmer 20
minutes. Turn into blender container;
cover and blend till smooth. Cool
slightly; stir in whipping cream. Cover
and chill. If desired, garnish with
sour cream and fresh mint. Makes 4
servings.

Cherry-Wine Soup

1 16-ounce can pitted tart
    red cherries
1½ cups water
½ cup sugar
1 tablespoon quick-cooking
    tapioca
⅛ teaspoon ground cloves
½ cup dry red wine

In 1½-quart saucepan stir together
undrained cherries, water, sugar,
tapioca, and cloves. Let stand 5 minutes. Bring to boiling. Reduce heat;
cover and simmer for 15 minutes, stirring occasionally. Remove from heat;
stir in wine. Cover and chill, stirring
occasionally. Makes 6 to 8 servings.

QUICK-SOUPS
COLD SOUPS

Cottage Cheese-Tomato Soup

2 cups tomato juice
1 cup cream-style cottage
    cheese
⅓ cup milk
2 teaspoons soy sauce
1 teaspoon worcestershire
    sauce
    Few drops bottled hot
    pepper sauce
2 tablespoons sliced green
    onion

In blender container combine
tomato juice, cottage cheese, milk,
soy sauce, worcestershire sauce,
and hot pepper sauce. Add *half* the
green onion. Cover and blend till
smooth. Cover and chill. Sprinkle
individual servings with the
remaining green onion. Makes
4 to 6 servings.

Pumpkin Bisque

1 16-ounce can pumpkin
⅓ cup sour cream dip with
    chives
2 cups chicken broth
    (see tip, page 87)
1 cup light cream
½ teaspoon salt

In a mixing bowl combine pumpkin,
sour cream dip, chicken broth,
cream, and salt; beat smooth with
rotary beater. Cover and chill. Garnish with dollops of additional sour
cream dip with chives, if desired.
Makes 6 to 8 servings.

Chilled Beet Soup

*Served in glasses, teacups, mugs, or
bowls, this ruby red soup makes a
perfect appetizer or snack for a warm
day. Garnish with lemon and green
onion as shown on page 25—*

1 16-ounce can diced beets
1 slice onion
1½ cups chicken broth
    (see tip, page 87)
1 tablespoon lemon juice
1 teaspoon sugar
½ teaspoon salt
¼ teaspoon pepper
    Dash ground cloves
    Lemon slices
    (optional)
    Sliced green onion
    (optional)

Combine the *undrained* beets and
onion slice in blender container or
food processor. Cover and blend till
very smooth. In large bowl combine
beet mixture, chicken broth, lemon
juice, sugar, salt, pepper, and ground
cloves; mix well.
    Cover and chill thoroughly. Serve
the soup in chilled bowls; top each
serving with lemon slices and green
onion, if desired. Makes 6 to 8
servings.

Blackberry Soup

1 16-ounce can blackberries
1 cup water
1 8-ounce carton lemon
    yogurt
½ cup grape juice
⅛ teaspoon ground cinnamon
1 small banana, sliced
2 tablespoons toasted
    coconut

Place *undrained* berries in blender
container or food processor; cover
and blend till smooth. Drain; discard
seeds. Return liquid to blender or
food processor; add water, yogurt,
grape juice, and cinnamon. Cover
and blend just till smooth. Cover and
chill. Garnish with banana slices and
toasted coconut. Makes 6 to 8
servings.

Appetizer Tomato Soup

1 10¾-ounce can condensed
    tomato soup
1¾ cups milk
1 8-ounce carton plain
    yogurt
1 teaspoon worcestershire
    sauce
¼ teaspoon celery salt
⅛ teaspoon onion powder

In bowl blend tomato soup, milk,
yogurt, worcestershire sauce, celery
salt, and onion powder. Cover; chill
thoroughly. Top each serving with
additional yogurt, if desired. Makes
6 servings.

Avocado Soup

1 13¾-ounce can chicken
   broth
2 medium avocados, seeded,
   peeled, and cut into
   chunks
2 tablespoons dry sherry
½ teaspoon salt
¼ teaspoon onion powder
⅛ teaspoon dried dillweed
¾ cup light cream

In blender container combine
chicken broth, avocado chunks, dry
sherry, salt, onion powder, and
dillweed. Cover; blend till mixture is
smooth. Stir in light cream. Cover;
chill well. Top each serving with
avocado slices or dollops of dairy
sour cream, if desired. Makes 6
servings.

Tomato Soup Shake

1 10¾-ounce can condensed
   tomato soup
1 cup light cream
1 egg (optional)
¼ teaspoon ground nutmeg
   Milk

Combine condensed soup, cream,
egg (if desired), and nutmeg in
blender container or shaker. Blend
or shake till smooth. Cover; chill.
Thin with a little milk, if necessary.
Serve in chilled cups or mugs. Makes
3 or 4 servings.

Orange-Apricot Soup

2 17-ounce cans apricot
   halves
1 teaspoon finely shredded
   orange peel
½ cup orange juice
¼ teaspoon ground cardamom
1 8-ounce carton plain
   yogurt

Drain apricots, reserving syrup.
In blender container place reserved
syrup and *half* the apricots. Add
orange peel, juice, and cardamom.
Cover and blend till smooth. Add
yogurt; blend just till combined.
Cut up remaining apricots; stir in.
Cover and chill. Garnish with orange
slices, if desired. Serves 8 to 10.

Shortcut Work with Appliances

*Put your kitchen appliances to
work and speed up soup-making
tasks. For instance, use a blender or food processor to puree,
chop, or blend foods. A food
processor can slice and shred
ingredients, as well.*

*A word of caution! Always read
and follow the information in
your appliances' use and care
booklets. Be aware of the type
and size of the food pieces
you're processing, as well as the
quantity that can be added to the
appliance container at one time.
You'll find that you may need to
process the food in batches to
prevent spills and overflow.*

Chilly Celery Soup

1 10¾-ounce can condensed
   cream of celery soup
1½ cups milk
2 tablespoons chopped green
   pepper
2 tablespoons diced pimiento
   Celery leaves

In blender container or food
processor place celery soup and
milk. Cover and blend till well
mixed. Add green pepper and
pimiento; cover and blend till
finely chopped. Cover and chill
thoroughly. Garnish each serving
with celery leaves. Makes 3 or 4
servings.

Cantaloupe Mist

1 medium cantaloupe
¼ teaspoon ground cinnamon
1 6-ounce can frozen orange
   juice concentrate
2 juice cans water (about
   1½ cups)
1 tablespoon lime juice

Cut cantaloupe in half and remove
seeds. Scoop pulp into blender
container or food processor. Add
cinnamon. Cover and blend till
smooth. Turn into large bowl. In
same blender container or food
processor place orange juice and
water. Cover and blend till mixed.
Stir into melon mixture; stir in lime
juice. Cover and chill thoroughly.
Stir before serving. Garnish with
fresh mint leaves or lime wedges,
if desired. Makes 6 to 8 servings.

WHOLE~MEAL SOUPS and STEWS

meat & poultry~fish & seafood~vegetable

Look to this chapter for main-dish soups and stews that can handle big or small appetites. First you'll find soups featuring beef, chicken, sausage, veal, lamb, and pork. Following these are plain and fancy soups that use fish and shellfish.

The vegetable section includes a selection of soups and stews that don't depend on meat for their protein power. Included are favorite bean, lentil, and pea soups.

Soup-bowl meals include (clockwise from the top) hearty Meaty Minestrone, easy-to-fix Salmon-Potato Chowder, and Vegetarian Chili. (See Index for recipe pages.)

MEAT AND POULTRY

Basic Stew

Use this recipe to make many stews by varying the meat, vegetables, and seasonings—

1½ pounds stew meat, cut into
    1-inch cubes (beef,
    pork, lamb, *or* veal)
2 tablespoons cooking oil
1 clove garlic, minced
1 bay leaf
1 teaspoon salt
1 teaspoon prepared mustard
    or prepared horseradish
½ teaspoon dried herb,
    crushed (basil, oregano,
    marjoram, *or* thyme)
¼ teaspoon pepper
1 10½- *or* 10¾-ounce can
    condensed broth (beef
    or chicken)
5 cups fresh vegetables cut
    into 1-inch pieces (any
    combination of peeled
    potatoes, carrots, cel-
    ery, rutabagas, turnips,
    onions, parsnips, *or*
    green peppers)
¼ cup cold water
2 tablespoons all-purpose
    flour

In large saucepan brown meat, *half* at a time, in hot oil. Return all meat to pan. Stir in garlic, bay leaf, salt, mustard or horseradish, herb, and pepper. Add the condensed beef or chicken broth. Bring to boiling. Reduce heat; cover and simmer till meat is nearly tender (about 30 minutes for pork, lamb, or veal; about 1¼ hours for beef). Add vegetables. Cover and simmer about 30 minutes or till meat and vegetables are tender. Blend water and flour; stir into stew. Cook and stir till thickened and bubbly. Remove bay leaf. Makes 6 servings.

Cider Stew

2 pounds beef stew meat, cut
    into 1-inch cubes
3 tablespoons all-purpose
    flour
2 teaspoons salt
¼ teaspoon pepper
¼ teaspoon dried thyme,
    crushed
3 tablespoons cooking oil
2 cups apple cider *or*
    apple juice
1 to 2 tablespoons vinegar
3 potatoes, peeled and
    quartered
4 carrots, quartered
2 onions, sliced
1 stalk celery, sliced

Coat meat with mixture of flour, salt, pepper, and thyme. In 4½-quart Dutch oven brown meat, *half* at a time, in hot oil. Drain off fat. Return all meat to Dutch oven. Stir in apple cider or juice, vinegar, and ½ cup *water*; cook and stir till mixture boils. Reduce heat; cover and simmer about 1¼ hours or till meat is nearly tender. Stir in vegetables. Cook 30 minutes more or till vegetables are done. Serves 6 to 8.

Crockery cooking directions: Use ingredients as listed above *except* add 1 *apple,* chopped; ½ cup cold *water;* and ¼ cup all-purpose *flour* as directed below. Coat meat with mixture of the 3 tablespoons flour, salt, pepper, and thyme. In skillet brown meat, *half* at a time, in hot oil. Drain off fat. Place vegetables and 1 *apple,* chopped, in electric slow crockery cooker. Place meat atop. Pour apple cider or juice and vinegar over meat. Cover and cook on low-heat setting for 10 to 12 hours. Turn cooker to high-heat setting. Blend ½ cup cold *water* and ¼ cup all-purpose *flour;* stir into stew. Cover and cook 15 minutes or till thickened. Season to taste.

Shaker Beef Goulash

This potato-topped beef stew is pictured on page 60—

2 tablespoons all-purpose
    flour
2 teaspoons salt
⅛ teaspoon pepper
2 pounds beef stew meat, cut
    into 1-inch cubes
2 tablespoons cooking oil
2 large onions, sliced
1 cup water
1 cup apple juice *or* cider
2 medium rutabagas, peeled
    and chopped (4 cups)
6 medium carrots, chopped
    (3 cups)
2 tablespoons snipped
    parsley
1 teaspoon salt
½ teaspoon dried marjoram,
    crushed
½ teaspoon dried thyme,
    crushed
⅓ cup cold water
3 tablespoons all-purpose
    flour
6 small potatoes, peeled,
    cooked, and mashed

In paper or plastic bag combine the 2 tablespoons flour, the 2 teaspoons salt, and the pepper. Add meat cubes, a few at a time, shaking to coat. In Dutch oven brown meat, *half* at a time, in hot oil. Return all meat to Dutch oven. Add onions, the 1 cup water, and apple juice. Cover and simmer about 1¼ hours or till meat is nearly tender. Add rutabagas, carrots, parsley, the 1 teaspoon salt, the marjoram, and thyme. Cover and simmer 30 minutes or till meat and vegetables are done. Blend the ⅓ cup water and the 3 tablespoons flour; stir into stew. Cook and stir till bubbly. Transfer to serving dish. Spoon potatoes around edge. Sprinkle with more parsley, if desired. Serves 8.

Chili Beef Soup

1½ pounds beef stew meat, cut
    into ½-inch cubes
2 tablespoons cooking oil
1 medium onion, chopped
    (½ cup)
1 medium green pepper,
    chopped (½ cup)
1 clove garlic, minced

• • •

3 cups water
1 18-ounce can (2¼ cups)
    tomato juice
1 16-ounce can tomatoes,
    cut up
1 16-ounce can whole kernel
    corn
1 15½-ounce can chili beans
2 bay leaves
1 tablespoon chili powder
2 teaspoons salt
1 teaspoon worcestershire
    sauce
¼ teaspoon pepper
¼ teaspoon crushed dried red
    pepper
½ cup cold water
⅓ cup all-purpose flour

In Dutch oven brown *half* the meat in hot oil; remove from pan. Brown the remaining meat with onion, green pepper, and garlic. Return all meat to pan. Add the 3 cups water, the tomato juice, *undrained* tomatoes, *undrained* corn, *undrained* chili beans, bay leaves, chili powder, salt, worcestershire sauce, pepper, and dried red pepper. Bring to boiling. Reduce heat; cover and simmer for 1½ to 2 hours or till meat is tender. Remove bay leaves.

Blend the ½ cup cold water and the flour. Stir into soup; cook and stir till slightly thickened and bubbly. Makes 8 servings.

Beef Stew with Ravioli Dumplings

3 tablespoons all-purpose
    flour
1 teaspoon salt
    Dash pepper
1 pound beef stew meat, cut
    into 1-inch cubes
2 tablespoons cooking oil
1 medium onion, chopped
    (½ cup)
1 clove garlic, minced
¾ teaspoon dried oregano,
    crushed
1 10-ounce package frozen
    peas and carrots
1 15-ounce can beef ravioli
    in sauce
2 tablespoons snipped
    parsley

In paper or plastic bag combine flour, salt, and pepper. Add *beef* cubes, a few at a time, shaking to coat. In skillet brown meat quickly in hot oil. Add onion, garlic, and oregano; cook till onion is tender. Drain off fat. Add 2½ cups *water*. Cover and simmer about 1¼ hours or till meat is nearly tender. In strainer rinse peas and carrots under hot water to separate; stir peas and carrots, ravioli, and parsley into stew. Cover and cook 20 minutes longer. Makes 4 servings.

Crockery cooking directions: (Use 3½-quart or smaller electric slow crockery cooker because of small volume.) Use ingredients as listed above. Coat beef with mixture of flour, salt, and pepper. In skillet brown meat in hot oil. Add onion, garlic, and oregano; cook till onion is tender. Transfer to electric slow crockery cooker. Add peas and carrots and 1½ cups *water*. Cover and cook on low-heat setting for 8 to 10 hours. Turn cooker to high-heat setting. Stir in ravioli and parsley. Cover and cook 15 minutes or till heated through.

Spiced Beef Stew

2 pounds beef stew meat, cut
    into 1-inch cubes
2 tablespoons cooking oil
2½ cups water
1 10½-ounce can *condensed*
    beef broth
2 bay leaves
2 teaspoons dried oregano,
    crushed
2 teaspoons ground coriander
1½ teaspoons salt
1 teaspoon ground cumin
¼ teaspoon pepper
1 clove garlic, minced
¾ cup cold water
½ cup all-purpose flour
3 medium sweet potatoes,
    peeled and cubed (about
    3 cups)
2 medium tomatoes, peeled
    and quartered
1 medium onion, cut into
    wedges
1 medium green pepper, cut
    into strips
½ small head cabbage, cut
    into wedges

In 4½-quart Dutch oven brown meat, *half* at a time, in hot oil. Return all meat to pan. Add the 2½ cups water, the condensed beef broth, bay leaves, oregano, coriander, salt, cumin, pepper, and garlic. Bring to boiling. Reduce heat; cover and simmer about 1¼ hours or till meat is nearly tender. Remove bay leaves; skim off fat. Blend together the ¾ cup water and flour; stir into meat mixture. Cook and stir till thickened and bubbly. Stir in sweet potatoes, tomatoes, onion, and green pepper; arrange cabbage atop. Cover and simmer about 20 minutes or till meat and vegetables are tender. Serves 8.

South American-style FISH SOUP (left rear) features white wine in a broth full of fish, potato, and tomato chunks. See recipe on page 68.

SOUTH AMERICAN PORK SOUP (left center) bursts with the color and flavor of beef and pork, as well as a variety of vegetables. See recipe on page 65.

Serve the meat and vegetables from ARGENTINA STEW (front) on a serving platter, and the broth in soup bowls. See recipe on page 46.

Beef flank steak simmers with vegetables and rice in BEEF SOUP (right). See recipe on page 38.

Flavored with beef ribs, PUMPKIN SOUP (center rear) is a full-bodied soup to serve as an appetizer or with a sandwich. See recipe on page 9.

Beef and Bean Ragout

1 cup dry dark red kidney
   beans
3 cups water
¼ cup all-purpose flour
½ teaspoon salt
2 pounds beef stew meat, cut
   into 1-inch cubes
2 tablespoons cooking oil
1 16-ounce can tomatoes,
   cut up
¾ cup dry red wine
2 cloves garlic, minced
1½ teaspoons salt
1 teaspoon sugar
½ teaspoon dried thyme,
   crushed
⅛ teaspoon pepper
1 bay leaf
3 medium potatoes, peeled
   and cubed (3 cups)
2 medium onions, cut into
   wedges
1 medium green pepper,
   chopped (½ cup)

Rinse beans. Place in 2-quart sauce-pan with the water; bring to boiling. Reduce heat and simmer 2 minutes. Remove from heat; cover and let stand 1 hour. (Or, combine beans and water; soak overnight.) Do not drain. Bring beans to boiling. Reduce heat, cover and simmer 45 minutes. Drain beans.

Combine flour and the ½ tea-spoon salt; coat meat with flour mix-ture. In 4-quart Dutch oven brown meat, half at a time, in hot oil. Return all meat to pan. Add drained beans, undrained tomatoes, wine, garlic, the 1½ teaspoons salt, the sugar, thyme, pepper, and bay leaf to the meat. Bring to boiling; reduce heat. Cover and simmer about 1¼ hours or till meat is nearly tender. Add potatoes, onions, and green pepper. Cook 30 minutes more or till meat and potatoes are tender. Remove bay leaf. Makes 8 to 10 servings.

Beef Soup

Use acorn, butternut, hubbard, or other winter squash in this distinctive soup pictured on page 36—

2 pounds beef flank steak
1 tablespoon lard or
   cooking oil
6 cups water
1 tablespoon salt
4 potatoes, peeled and
   quartered
2 carrots, cut into 1-inch
   pieces
2 onions, quartered
8 ounces winter squash or
   pumpkin, peeled and cut
   into 8 pieces
2 ears fresh corn, quartered
1 cup sliced fresh green
   beans
¼ cup long grain rice
¼ cup chopped celery leaves
¼ cup snipped parsley
2 cloves garlic, minced
¼ teaspoon ground white
   pepper
⅛ teaspoon crushed dried
   red pepper

Cut meat into 8 pieces. In 5-quart Dutch oven brown meat, half at a time, in hot lard or cooking oil. Re-turn all meat to pan; add the water and salt. Bring mixture to boiling. Reduce heat; cover and simmer about 1¼ hours or till meat is nearly tender. Add potatoes, carrots, on-ions, squash or pumpkin, corn, beans, uncooked rice, celery leaves, parsley, garlic, white pepper, and red pepper. Cover and simmer about 30 minutes or till vegetables are tender. Remove meat and vegetables to plat-ter. Divide broth among 8 soup plates; add ingredients from platter. Makes 8 servings.

Succotash Soup

1½ pounds corned beef brisket
1 medium carrot, chopped
   (½ cup)
1 stalk celery, chopped
   (½ cup)
8 cups water
1 2½- to 3-pound broiler-
   fryer chicken, cut up
2 medium potatoes, peeled
   and chopped (2 cups)
2 cups fresh lima beans or
   1 10-ounce package
   frozen lima beans
1 medium onion, chopped
   (½ cup)
½ teaspoon dried sage,
   crushed
¼ teaspoon pepper
4 ears corn or 1 10-ounce
   package frozen whole
   kernel corn

In 5-quart Dutch oven combine beef, carrot, and celery. Add water; bring to boiling. Reduce heat; cover and simmer for 1½ hours. Add chicken pieces; simmer, covered, for 45 to 50 minutes or till beef and chicken are tender. Remove beef and chicken; strain broth, discarding, vegetables. Spoon fat from broth. Cool beef and chicken slightly. Remove and discard skin and bones from chicken. Cut up beef and chicken; set aside. Add potatoes, lima beans, onion, sage, and pepper to broth. Cover and simmer about 20 minutes or till limas are almost tender. Cut fresh corn from cobs. Stir fresh or frozen corn, beef, and chicken into soup. Return to boil. Cover and simmer about 15 minutes or till vegetables are tender. Season to taste with salt and pepper. Makes 8 to 10 servings.

Beef and Kraut Soup

2 pounds beef shank
   crosscuts
2 tablespoons cooking oil
1 medium onion, chopped
   (½ cup)
1 clove garlic, minced
4 whole cloves
1 bay leaf
2 teaspoons salt
⅛ teaspoon pepper
1 8-ounce can sauerkraut,
   snipped
1 8-ounce can tomatoes,
   cut up
1 medium apple, peeled,
   cored, and chopped
1 green pepper, chopped
   (½ cup)
1 teaspoon sugar

In Dutch oven brown beef in hot oil. Remove from pan; add onion and garlic to drippings and cook till onion is tender. Return beef to pan. Add cloves, bay leaf, salt, pepper, and 4 cups *water.* Cover and simmer for 1½ hours. Remove beef. Remove bay leaf and cloves. When cool enough to handle, remove meat from bones; cut up meat and return to broth. Discard bones. Stir in *undrained* sauerkraut, *undrained* tomatoes, apple, green pepper, and sugar. Bring to boiling; reduce heat. Cover and simmer 15 to 20 minutes more or till pepper is tender. Top with sour cream, if desired. Makes 6 servings.

Crockery cooking directions: Use ingredients as listed above. In skillet brown beef in oil; drain. Transfer beef to electric slow crockery cooker. Combine remaining ingredients and 3 cups *water.* Pour mixture over beef in cooker. Cover and cook on low-heat setting about 10 hours. Remove beef; skim off any fat. Remove bay leaf and cloves. Remove meat from bones; cut up meat and return to soup. Discard bones.

Short Rib-Vegetable Stew

2 pounds beef short ribs,
   cut into serving-size
   pieces
1 tablespoon cooking oil
1 16-ounce can tomatoes,
   cut up
1 medium onion, chopped
   (½ cup)
1 clove garlic, minced
1½ teaspoons salt
1½ teaspoons instant
   vegetable bouillon
   granules
½ teaspoon dried basil,
   crushed
   Dash pepper
1 pound tiny new potatoes
   (10 to 12)
3 carrots, cut into ½-inch
   pieces
1 8½-ounce can peas, drained
1 8½-ounce can lima beans,
   drained
2 tablespoons snipped
   parsley

Trim excess fat from ribs. In Dutch oven slowly brown ribs in hot oil on all sides; drain off fat. Add *undrained* tomatoes, onion, garlic, salt, bouillon granules, basil, and pepper. Add 2½ cups *water.* Bring to boiling. Reduce heat; cover and simmer for 2 hours or till meat is nearly tender. Skim off fat.

Peel strip around center of each potato, if desired. Add potatoes, carrots, drained peas, drained lima beans, and parsley to Dutch oven. Cover and simmer about 30 minutes more or till vegetables are tender. Season to taste with salt and pepper. Makes 6 servings.

Crockery cooking directions: Use ingredients as listed above. Trim excess fat from ribs. In skillet slowly brown ribs in hot oil on all sides; drain well. Combine *undrained* tomatoes, garlic, salt, bouillon granules, basil, and pepper. Set aside. Peel strip

around center of each potato, if desired. Place potatoes, carrots, onion, peas, limas, and parsley in electric slow crockery cooker. Add browned ribs. Pour tomato mixture over meat in cooker. Add 2 cups *water;* do not stir. Cover and cook on low-heat setting for 8 hours. Skim off excess fat. Season to taste.

Crockery Cooker Hints

Electric slow crockery cookers come in three basic types: 1) cookers with heating wires wrapped entirely around the sides of the cooker, 2) cookers with heating elements in the bottom, and 3) cookers with a separate heating unit.

Cooking characteristics vary with each type, and we found that our recipes developed for unattended long-term cooking were satisfactory only when done in the first kind of cooker.

All the crockery cooking directions given in this book were tested only in cookers with heating elements wrapped around the sides. These pots have very low wattage and their heating element is on continuously. Foods in liquid can be left unattended for 8 or more hours without boiling dry or sticking. This group of pots can be identified by its heat control with one or two fixed settings, usually low and high.

Most of the recipe directions specify the low-heat setting. However, if you want to reduce the cooking time, most foods cook on the high-heat setting in half the time they require on the low-heat setting.

Meaty Minestrone

- 3 pounds beef shank crosscuts
- 1 medium onion, chopped (½ cup)
- 1 bay leaf
- 2 teaspoons salt
- ¼ teaspoon pepper
- 8 cups water
- 1 16-ounce can cut green beans, drained
- 1 15-ounce can garbanzo beans, drained
- 1 8-ounce can tomatoes, cut up
- 2 medium carrots, thinly sliced (1 cup)
- 4 ounces Polish sausage, thinly sliced
- 2 ounces fine noodles (1¼ cups)
- 2 tablespoons snipped parsley
- 1 clove garlic, minced
- 1½ teaspoons dried basil, crushed
- Grated parmesan cheese (optional)

In Dutch oven combine beef, onion, bay leaf, salt, and pepper. Add water. Cover and simmer about 1½ hours or till meat is tender. Remove beef; skim fat from broth. When meat is cool enough to handle, remove meat from bones; cut up meat and return to broth. Discard bones. Add green beans, garbanzo beans, *undrained* tomatoes, carrots, sausage, noodles, parsley, garlic, and basil to soup. Cover and simmer for 20 to 25 minutes or till vegetables and noodles are tender. Remove bay leaf; season to taste. If desired, pass grated parmesan cheese. Makes 8 to 10 servings.

Beef Stew with Wontons

Beef Stew with Wontons

- 1½ pounds beef stew meat, cut into 1-inch cubes
- 1 medium onion, chopped (½ cup)
- 1 clove garlic, minced
- 2 tablespoons cooking oil
- ½ cup dry white wine
- ¼ cup soy sauce
- 2 teaspoons instant beef bouillon granules
- 2 teaspoons sugar
- ½ teaspoon ground ginger
  Wontons (see recipe below)
- 3 cups coarsely chopped bok choy
- 1 cup sliced fresh mushrooms
- 1 6-ounce package frozen pea pods
- ¼ cup cornstarch

In 4-quart Dutch oven cook meat, onion, and garlic, *half* at a time, in oil till meat is brown. Return all to pan. Add wine, soy, bouillon granules, sugar, ginger, and 3½ cups *water*. Bring to boiling; reduce heat. Cover and simmer 1½ hours or till meat is tender; stir occasionally. Meanwhile, prepare Wontons.

Add bok choy, mushrooms, and pea pods to stew; simmer 2 or 3 minutes. Blend cornstarch and ¼ cup cold *water*; stir into hot mixture. Cook and stir till thickened and bubbly. Add hot Wontons. Serves 6 to 8.

Wontons

- 1 4½-ounce can shrimp
- 1 beaten egg yolk
- ½ cup finely chopped bok choy
- ¼ cup finely chopped onion
- 1 tablespoon soy sauce
- ½ teaspoon sugar
- ¼ teaspoon ground ginger
- 20 wonton skins

Drain, devein, and chop shrimp. Combine shrimp, egg yolk, bok choy, onion, soy, sugar, ginger, ¼ teaspoon *salt*, and ⅛ teaspoon *pepper*. Follow directions below for filling and wrapping wontons. In large saucepan cook wontons in a large amount of boiling water for 3 to 5 minutes. Drain. Add to stew (see recipe at left).

Wrapping Wontons

Buy wonton skins at the supermarket or Oriental food store. If wonton skins are not available, purchase egg roll skins and cut each in quarters.

Position wonton skin with one point toward you. Spoon a scant tablespoonful of filling just off center of skin. Fold bottom

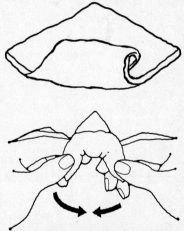

point of wonton skin over filling; tuck point under filling, leaving about 1 inch unrolled at top of skin. Moisten right-hand corner of skin with water. Grasp right- and left-hand corners as shown; bring these corners toward you below the filling. Overlap left-hand corner over right-hand corner; press to seal.

Easy Vegetable-Beef Soup

Soup mix and frozen vegetables save you time when making this tasty soup, pictured on page 44—

5 cups water
1½ pounds beef shank crosscuts
1 16-ounce can tomatoes, cut up
1 10-ounce package frozen mixed vegetables
1 cup frozen loose-pack hash brown potatoes
¼ cup *regular* onion soup mix
¼ cup sliced celery
1 teaspoon sugar
1 teaspoon seasoned salt
½ teaspoon worcestershire sauce
⅛ teaspoon pepper
    Dash bottled hot pepper sauce

In 3-quart saucepan combine water and beef; bring to boiling. Reduce heat; cover and simmer for 1½ to 2 hours or till meat is tender. Skim off fat. (Or, chill beef and broth till layer of fat forms; remove and discard fat.) Remove meat. Measure the cooking liquid; reserve 3 cups of the liquid to use in soup (save remaining cooking liquid for another use). When the meat is cool enough to handle, re-move meat from bones; cut meat into bite-size pieces. Discard bones.

In saucepan combine the 3 cups reserved liquid, the meat, *undrained* tomatoes, mixed vegetables, pota-toes, dry onion soup mix, celery, sugar, seasoned salt, worcestershire sauce, pepper, and hot pepper sauce. Bring to boiling. Reduce heat; cover and simmer for 15 to 20 minutes or till vegetables are tender. Serves 6.

Oxtail Vegetable Soup

Choose the meatiest oxtails for this hearty soup, shown on page 44—

2 pounds oxtails, cut into 1½-inch lengths
3 tablespoons all-purpose flour
2 tablespoons cooking oil
1 16-ounce can tomatoes, cut up
1 10½-ounce can *condensed* beef broth
½ cup water
½ cup dry red wine
1 medium onion, chopped (½ cup)
1 teaspoon sugar
½ teaspoon salt
½ teaspoon dried thyme, crushed
¼ teaspoon pepper
1 bay leaf
4 medium carrots, cut into julienne strips (2 cups)
4 medium parsnips, peeled and cut into julienne strips (2 cups)
½ cup frozen peas

Trim fat from oxtails. Coat oxtails with flour. In Dutch oven brown oxtails in hot oil. Add *undrained* tomatoes, condensed beef broth, water, wine, onion, sugar, salt, thyme, pepper, and bay leaf. Bring to boiling. Reduce heat; cover and simmer 2 hours or till meat is just tender. Skim off fat. Add carrots and parsnips; cover and sim-mer 25 minutes. Stir in peas; cook 5 minutes more. Serve in soup plates. Makes 4 servings.

Onion Oxtail Stew

⅓ cup all-purpose flour
1 teaspoon salt
    Dash pepper
5 pounds oxtails, cut into 1½-inch lengths
¼ cup cooking oil
1 10½-ounce can *condensed* beef broth
1 cup water
1 cup dry white wine
1 large onion, chopped (1 cup)
1 tomato, peeled and chopped
1 large carrot, finely chopped
1 medium turnip, peeled and finely chopped (1 cup)
2 cloves garlic, minced
    Few sprigs parsley
1 bay leaf
½ teaspoon salt
    Dash pepper
2 cups pearl onions *or* frozen small whole onions
3 medium carrots, sliced (1½ cups)

Combine the flour, the 1 teaspoon salt, and dash pepper. Coat oxtails with flour mixture. In 10-quart Dutch oven slowly brown oxtails, *half* at a time, in hot oil, turning often; drain off excess fat. Return all meat to pan. Add condensed beef broth, water, ½ *cup* of the wine, the chopped onion, tomato, the chopped carrot, turnip, garlic, parsley, and bay leaf. Bring to boiling. Reduce heat; cover and simmer 1½ hours. Remove and dis-card parsley and bay leaf. Skim off fat. Return to boiling; reduce heat and stir in remaining ½ cup wine, the ½ teaspoon salt, and dash pepper. Cover and simmer for 30 minutes. Add pearl onions and sliced carrots; cover and simmer 20 to 25 minutes more. Makes 5 to 8 servings.

Oven-Style Borscht Stew

2 pounds beef short ribs,
   cut up
1 tablespoon cooking oil
4 medium carrots, sliced
   (2 cups)
3 medium turnips, peeled
   and cut into julienne
   strips
2 stalks celery, sliced
   (1 cup)
1 large onion, sliced
4 cups water
1 6-ounce can tomato paste
1 tablespoon salt
¼ teaspoon pepper
   • • •
1 cup water
1 tablespoon sugar
1 tablespoon vinegar
2 medium beets, peeled and
   cut into julienne strips
1 small head cabbage, cut
   into 6 wedges
   Dairy sour cream

In 4½-quart Dutch oven brown short ribs in hot oil. Drain off fat. Add carrots, turnips, celery, and onion. Combine the 4 cups water, the tomato paste, salt, and pepper; pour over vegetables in Dutch oven. Cover and bake in 350° oven for 2 hours. Skim off fat.

Combine the 1 cup water, the sugar, and vinegar; add to meat mixture. Add beets; place cabbage atop mixture, pushing partially into liquid. Cover and continue baking 1½ hours more. Serve in soup plates. Pass sour cream to spoon atop each serving. Makes 6 servings.

Oven-Baked Beef Stew

¼ cup all-purpose flour
2 teaspoons salt
⅛ teaspoon pepper
1½ pounds beef stew meat, cut
   into 1-inch cubes
3 or 4 medium carrots, cut
   into 2-inch strips
4 small onions, quartered
2 cups water
1 6-ounce can tomato paste
1 tablespoon vinegar
1 teaspoon sugar
⅛ teaspoon dried thyme,
   crushed
1 clove garlic, minced
1 bay leaf
1 10-ounce package frozen
   peas, broken apart
1 package refrigerated
   biscuits (6 biscuits)
   Milk
¼ cup crisp rice cereal,
   crushed

In paper or plastic bag combine flour, salt, and pepper. Add beef cubes, a few at a time; shake to coat. Place coated beef cubes in a 2½- to 3-quart casserole; add carrots and onions. In bowl combine water, tomato paste, vinegar, sugar, thyme, garlic, and bay leaf; pour over meat mixture in casserole. Bake, covered, in 350° oven for 2 hours.

Stir frozen peas into stew mixture; cover and bake 20 minutes longer. Remove casserole from oven; discard bay leaf. Increase oven temperature to 425°.

Meanwhile, quarter the refrigerated biscuits; dip each quarter in milk, then roll in cereal. Place atop hot stew. Bake, uncovered, in 425° oven about 12 minutes or till biscuits are done. Makes 6 servings.

Meatball Stew with Spinach Dumplings

1 beaten egg
¾ cup soft bread crumbs
   (1 slice)
1 teaspoon garlic salt
1 pound ground beef
1 tablespoon cooking oil
1 medium onion, chopped
   (½ cup)
1 11-ounce can condensed
   cheddar cheese soup
1 soup can milk (1¼ cups)
1 16-ounce can diced beets,
   drained
1 10-ounce package frozen
   brussels sprouts
1 8-ounce can spinach, well-
   drained and chopped
1 cup packaged biscuit mix
¼ cup milk

Mix egg, crumbs, and garlic salt. Add beef; mix well. Shape meat mixture into 1-inch meatballs. In 12-inch skillet brown meatballs in hot oil. Add onion; cook 5 minutes. Drain off fat. Combine cheese soup and the soup can of milk; add to skillet. Cover; simmer 10 minutes. Add beets and sprouts. Cover; simmer 5 minutes. Stir together spinach, biscuit mix, and the ¼ cup milk. Drop spinach mixture atop soup mixture to make eight dumplings. Cover; simmer 10 minutes. Makes 4 servings.

Shaping Meatballs

To shape uniform 1-inch meatballs, try one of these two methods. Form meat mixture into a roll 1 inch in diameter. Cut into 1-inch slices. Round each slice into a ball.

Or, pat meat mixture to a 1-inch-thick square; cut into 1-inch cubes. Round each cube into a ball.

Mound bulgur wheat atop LENTIL-PEPPERONI SOUP (left rear) for a special lentil soup. See recipe on page 82.

OXTAIL VEGETABLE SOUP (left front) makes scrumptious use of low-cost oxtails. See recipe on page 42.

HOT AND HEARTY HAM SOUP (center front) is served with double-cheese-topped rye toast. See recipe on page 63.

The full flavor of EASY VEGE-TABLE-BEEF SOUP (right front) won't betray how easy it is to make. See recipe on page 42.

Ladle PORK AND CABBAGE SOUP (right rear) from a tureen and garnish each serving with a spoonful of sour cream. See recipe on page 64.

Argentina Stew

Serve the meat and vegetables on a platter, as shown on page 36—

1 to 1½ pounds beef short
  ribs, cut into serving-
  size pieces
5 cups water
2 ounces lean salt pork,
  sliced (½ cup)
1½ teaspoons salt
⅛ teaspoon pepper
1 2½- to 3-pound broiler-
  fryer chicken, cut up
3 carrots, quartered
3 medium onions, quartered
3 tomatoes, quartered
3 medium potatoes, peeled
  and quartered (1 pound)
½ small head cabbage, cut
  into wedges
6 ounces winter squash *or*
  pumpkin, peeled and cut
  into 1-inch cubes (1 cup)
1 medium green pepper,
  chopped (½ cup)
3 tablespoons snipped
  parsley
1 clove garlic, minced

In 5-quart Dutch oven combine ribs, water, salt pork, salt, and pepper. Bring to boiling. Reduce heat; cover and simmer 1 hour. Add chicken; cover and simmer 25 minutes more. Add carrots, onions, tomatoes, potatoes, cabbage, squash or pumpkin, green pepper, parsley, and garlic; cover and simmer 20 minutes more or till vegetables are tender. Spoon off fat. (Or, cool slightly. Refrigerate several hours or overnight. Lift fat from surface. Return mixture to heat. Bring to boiling.) Season to taste with salt and pepper. Remove meat and vegetables from Dutch oven; arrange on platter. Garnish with additional parsley, if desired. Serve with bowls of broth. Makes 6 servings.

Booya

2 cups water
1 tablespoon salt
1 teaspoon dried oregano,
  crushed
1 teaspoon paprika
½ teaspoon dried savory,
  crushed
¼ teaspoon garlic salt
1 cup parsley sprigs
1 pound beef short ribs
½ pound boneless pork, cut
  into ½-inch cubes
½ pound beef stew meat, cut
  into ½-inch cubes
1 28-ounce can tomatoes,
  cut up
1 large onion, sliced
1 cup chopped red cabbage
2 medium carrots, chopped
  (1 cup)
1 cup chopped rutabaga
2 stalks celery, chopped
  (1 cup)
¼ cup chopped green pepper
1 16-ounce can cut green
  beans
1 8½-ounce can peas
1 8-ounce can whole kernel
  corn

In very large kettle or Dutch oven combine water, salt, oregano, paprika, savory, garlic salt, and parsley sprigs. Add ribs, pork, beef, *undrained* tomatoes, onion, cabbage, carrots, rutabaga, celery, and green pepper. Bring to boiling. Reduce heat; cover and simmer about 2 hours or till meat is nearly tender. Remove ribs from soup. When cool enough to handle, remove meat from bones and cube; discard bones. Return meat to kettle; add *undrained* green beans, *undrained* peas, and *undrained* corn. Cover and simmer 30 minutes. Makes 8 to 10 servings.
Crockery cooking directions: Use ingredients as listed above *except* add 2 tablespoons *cooking oil* as follows. In skillet brown ribs, pork, and

beef in the 2 tablespoons oil; drain off fat. Place the *undrained* tomatoes, onion, cabbage, carrots, rutabaga, celery, and green pepper in an electric slow crockery cooker. Place meat atop vegetables. Stir together water, salt, oregano, paprika, savory, garlic salt, and parsley; add to cooker. Cover and cook on low-heat setting for 10 to 12 hours. Remove meat from bones and cube; discard bones. Return meat to cooker; turn to high-heat setting. Add *undrained* beans, *undrained* peas, and *undrained* corn. Cover and cook for 1 hour.

Spanish Beef Soup

1 pound ground beef
¾ teaspoon salt
⅛ teaspoon pepper
1 15-ounce can tomato herb
  sauce
1 8-ounce can stewed onions,
  drained
2 medium carrots, cut into
  ½-inch pieces (1 cup)
1 3-ounce can sliced
  mushrooms
¼ cup sliced pimiento-
  stuffed olives
2½ cups water
½ cup dry red wine *or* water
  Grated parmesan cheese
  (optional)

In large saucepan cook ground beef till browned; drain off fat. Sprinkle meat with salt and pepper. Add tomato herb sauce, onions, carrots, *undrained* mushrooms, and olives. Stir in water and wine. Cover and simmer 30 to 35 minutes or till carrots are tender, stirring occasionally. Sprinkle with parmesan, if desired. Makes 6 servings.

Spicy Hot Chili

1 pound ground beef *or* ground pork
1 medium onion, chopped (½ cup)
2 cloves garlic, minced
1 16-ounce can tomatoes, cut up
1 16-ounce can red kidney beans, drained
¾ cup tomato juice
1 4-ounce can green chili peppers, rinsed, seeded, and chopped
1 tablespoon worcestershire sauce
2 teaspoons paprika
1 teaspoon sugar
1 teaspoon salt
1 teaspoon dried oregano, crushed
½ teaspoon ground cumin
¼ teaspoon celery salt
¼ teaspoon cayenne
¼ teaspoon pepper
⅛ teaspoon dry mustard
Few drops bottled hot pepper sauce

In large saucepan cook meat, onion, and garlic till meat is browned; drain off fat. Stir in *undrained* tomatoes, beans, tomato juice, chili peppers, worcestershire, paprika, sugar, salt, oregano, cumin, celery salt, cayenne, pepper, mustard, hot pepper sauce, and 1 cup *water*. Cover and simmer for 20 to 30 minutes. Makes 4 to 6 servings.

Crockery cooking directions: (Use a 3½-quart or smaller electric slow crockery cooker due to the small volume of chili.) Use ingredients as listed above. In skillet cook meat, onion, and garlic till meat is browned; drain off fat. Transfer meat mixture to electric slow crockery cooker. Stir in remaining ingredients, and ½ cup *water*. Cover and cook on low-heat setting for 8 to 10 hours.

Beef Goulash Soup

4 slices bacon
2 medium onions, chopped
2 cloves garlic, minced
1 to 1½ tablespoons paprika
2 teaspoons salt
2 pounds beef stew meat, cut into 1-inch cubes
1 medium tomato, cut up
1 6-ounce can tomato paste
3 medium potatoes, peeled and finely chopped

In Dutch oven cook bacon till crisp. Drain, reserving drippings; crumble bacon. Cook onions and garlic in reserved drippings till tender. Stir in paprika and salt. Add meat cubes and bacon; cook and stir 2 to 3 minutes. Add tomato, tomato paste, and 2 cups *water*. Cover and simmer 1¼ hours or till meat is nearly tender. Add potatoes. Simmer 20 minutes. Spoon off fat. Serves 6.

Hamburger Soup

1 pound ground beef
1 16-ounce can tomatoes, cut up
2 medium onions, chopped
2 medium carrots, sliced
2 stalks celery, chopped
⅓ cup pearl barley
¼ cup catsup
1 tablespoon instant beef bouillon granules
2 teaspoons seasoned salt
1 teaspoon dried basil, crushed
1 bay leaf

In large saucepan cook ground beef till browned. Drain off fat. Stir in remaining ingredients and 5 cups *water*. Bring to boiling. Reduce heat; cover and simmer for 1 hour. Season to taste with salt and pepper. Remove bay leaf. Serves 6.

Beef and Beer-Vegetable Soup

1 pound ground beef
1 medium onion, chopped (½ cup)
1 12-ounce can beer
1 10½-ounce can *condensed* beef broth
1 soup can water (1¼ cups)
3 medium carrots, thinly sliced (1½ cups)
1 medium turnip, chopped (about 1 cup)
1 stalk celery, thinly sliced (½ cup)
1 4-ounce can mushroom stems and pieces
1 bay leaf
1 teaspoon salt
⅛ teaspoon pepper
⅛ teaspoon ground allspice

In large saucepan cook ground beef and onion till meat is browned; drain off fat. Stir in beer, condensed beef broth, water, carrots, turnip, celery, *undrained* mushrooms, bay leaf, salt, pepper, and allspice. Bring to boiling. Reduce heat; cover and simmer for 30 to 35 minutes or till vegetables are tender. Remove bay leaf. Makes 4 to 6 servings.

Crockery cooking directions: Use ingredients as listed above. In skillet brown meat and onion; drain off fat. Transfer meat and onion to electric slow crockery cooker. Stir in beer, condensed beef broth, water, carrots, turnip, celery, *undrained* mushrooms, bay leaf, salt, pepper, and allspice. Cover and cook on low-heat setting for 8 to 10 hours or till vegetables are tender. Remove bay leaf.

Deviled Chicken Soup

1 3-pound broiler-fryer chicken, cut up
1 medium onion, chopped (½ cup)
1 stalk celery, chopped (½ cup)
1 teaspoon salt
¼ teaspoon pepper
1 18-ounce can (2¼ cups) tomato juice
1 16-ounce can cream-style corn
1 large potato, peeled and chopped (1½ cups)
2 tablespoons prepared mustard
1 teaspoon worcestershire sauce
½ teaspoon chili powder
⅛ teaspoon garlic powder
Dash cayenne

In a large kettle combine chicken pieces, onion, celery, salt, and pepper. Add 3 cups *water;* bring to boiling. Reduce heat; cover and simmer about 1 hour or till chicken is tender. Remove chicken from broth. Skim fat from broth. When chicken is cool enough to handle, remove the skin and bones from chicken; discard skin and bones. Cube chicken; set aside.

Stir tomato juice, corn, potato, mustard, worcestershire sauce, chili powder, garlic powder, and cayenne into the broth. Bring to boiling. Reduce heat; cover and simmer for 15 to 20 minutes or till potatoes are nearly tender. Stir in the cubed chicken. Cover and simmer about 5 minutes or till heated through. Season to taste with salt and pepper. Makes 6 servings.

Crockery cooking directions: Use ingredients as listed above. If desired, discard fat and skin from chicken pieces. Combine all ingredients in electric slow crockery cooker. Add 2½ cups *water.* Cover and cook on low-heat setting for 8 hours. Remove chicken with a slotted spoon. Skim fat from broth. When chicken is cool enough to handle, remove skin and bones from chicken; discard skin and bones. Cube chicken; return to soup. Heat through. Season to taste with salt and pepper.

Brunswick Stew

1 2½- to 3-pound broiler-fryer chicken, cut up
6 cups water
1½ teaspoons salt
1 teaspoon dried rosemary, crushed
1 bay leaf
2 medium potatoes, peeled and diced (2 cups)
1 16-ounce can tomatoes, cut up
1 16-ounce can cream-style corn
1 10-ounce package frozen cut okra
1 10-ounce package frozen lima beans
1 large onion, chopped (1 cup)
1 tablespoon sugar
1½ teaspoons salt
½ teaspoon pepper

Place chicken in 5-quart Dutch oven. Add water, 1½ teaspoons salt. rosemary, and bay leaf. Bring to boiling. Reduce heat; cover and simmer about 1 hour or till chicken is tender. Remove chicken from broth. Skim fat from broth. When chicken is cool enough to handle, remove skin and bones from chicken; discard skin and bones. Cut up chicken. Return cut-up chicken to broth. Stir in potatoes, *undrained* tomatoes, corn, okra, beans, onion, sugar, 1½ teaspoons salt, and pepper. Cover and simmer 40 minutes. Remove bay leaf. Makes 8 to 10 servings.

Meaty Basque Vegetable Soup

1 cup dry navy beans
7 cups water
1 2½- to 3-pound broiler-fryer chicken, cut up
1½ teaspoons salt
12 ounces Polish sausage, sliced
2 leeks, sliced
2 medium carrots, sliced (1 cup)
1 cup coarsely shredded cabbage
1 medium potato, peeled and cubed (1 cup)
1 medium turnip, peeled and cubed (1 cup)
1 medium onion, chopped (½ cup)
1 clove garlic, minced
1 tablespoon snipped parsley
1 teaspoon dried thyme, crushed
Croutons (optional)

Rinse beans. In Dutch oven or large saucepan, place beans and the water. Bring to boiling; cook 2 minutes. Remove from heat; cover and let stand 1 hour. (Or, combine beans and water; soak overnight.) *Do not drain.* Add chicken pieces and salt. Bring to boiling. Reduce heat; cover and simmer 1 hour.

Remove chicken from bean mixture. When chicken is cool enough to handle, remove skin and bones from chicken; discard skin and bones. Cut up chicken; stir into bean mixture. Stir in Polish sausage, leeks, carrots, cabbage, potato, turnip, onion, garlic, parsley, and thyme. Simmer 30 minutes more or till vegetables are tender. Ladle into bowls; sprinkle with croutons, if desired. Makes 8 servings.

Chicken-Vegetable Stew with Dumplings

2   2½- to 3-pound broiler-
    fryer chickens, cut up
4   cups water
3   stalks celery, chopped
    (1½ cups)
3   medium carrots, chopped
    (1½ cups)
3   medium onions, chopped
    (1½ cups)
1   tablespoon salt
1½ teaspoons dried thyme,
    crushed
¼   teaspoon pepper
1   cup cold water
½   cup all-purpose flour
1   10-ounce package frozen
    peas
1   4-ounce can mushroom
    stems and pieces
    Herb Dumplings (see
    recipe, page 91)
2   tablespoons snipped
    parsley

In Dutch oven or kettle place chicken pieces. Add the 4 cups water, celery, carrots, onions, salt, thyme, and pepper. Bring to boiling. Reduce heat; cover and simmer for 35 to 45 minutes or till chicken is nearly tender. Skim off fat.

Blend the 1 cup cold water and the flour; stir into chicken mixture. Stir in frozen peas and *undrained* mushrooms. Cook, stirring gently, till thickened and bubbly. Drop Herb Dumpling dough from tablespoon to make 8 mounds atop bubbling stew. Cover and simmer 15 minutes (do not lift cover). Sprinkle chicken and dumplings with the snipped parsley. Makes 8 servings.

Broccoli-Chicken Stew

12 chicken thighs, skinned
    (about 3 pounds)
2   tablespoons cooking oil
1   0.6-ounce envelope Italian
    salad dressing mix
1   teaspoon salt
3   cups water
½   cup dry white wine
½   cup catsup
    • • •
3   medium potatoes, peeled
    and cubed (3 cups)
2   cups frozen small whole
    onions (½ of a 20-ounce
    package)
1   10-ounce package frozen
    cut broccoli
1   medium green pepper, cut
    into cubes
2   cups sliced fresh
    mushrooms (5 ounces)
⅓   cup cold water
3   tablespoons all-purpose
    flour

In 4½-quart Dutch oven slowly brown chicken thighs, *half* at a time, in the hot oil. Remove chicken; drain fat from pan. In same Dutch oven combine dry salad dressing mix and salt. Stir in the 3 cups water, wine, and catsup. Return the browned chicken thighs to pan. Bring to boiling. Reduce heat; cover and simmer for 15 minutes.

Add potatoes and frozen onions. Simmer, covered, 15 minutes longer. Add frozen broccoli, the green pepper, and mushrooms. Cover and simmer 5 to 10 minutes longer or till vegetables are tender. Blend the ⅓ cup cold water and the flour; stir into stew. Cook and stir till thickened and bubbly. Makes 6 servings.

Chicken Vegetable-Noodle Soup

Tomatoes, corn, zucchini, and home-made noodles make this a company-special chicken soup—

6   cups water
1   5- to 6-pound stewing
    chicken, cut up
⅓   cup chopped onion
2   teaspoons salt
¼   teaspoon pepper
1   bay leaf
1   16-ounce can tomatoes,
    cut up
1   16-ounce can cream-style
    corn
2   small zucchini, thinly
    sliced (about 2 cups)
1½ cups uncooked Homemade
    Noodles (see recipe,
    page 89)

In a large kettle combine water, chicken pieces, chopped onion, salt, pepper, and bay leaf. Bring to boiling; reduce heat. Cover and simmer about 2 hours or till chicken is tender. Remove chicken from broth. Skim fat from broth; remove bay leaf. When chicken is cool enough to handle, remove skin and bones from chicken; discard skin and bones. Cube chicken; set aside.

Add *undrained* tomatoes, cream-style corn, and thinly sliced zucchini to broth. Bring mixture to boiling. Stir in Homemade Noodles. Cover and simmer about 8 minutes or till noodles are nearly tender. Stir in the cubed chicken. Cover and simmer about 5 minutes more or till heated through. Season to taste with salt and pepper. Makes 8 servings.

QUICK·SOUPS

MEAT AND POULTRY

Smoky Beef Chowder

For a change, use thinly sliced ham, pastrami, corned beef, or smoked turkey in this soup—

1 stalk celery, finely
   chopped (½ cup)
1 medium onion, finely
   chopped (½ cup)
2 tablespoons butter *or*
   margarine
3 tablespoons all-purpose
   flour
¼ teaspoon salt
¼ teaspoon dried basil,
   crushed
1 3-ounce package thinly
   sliced smoked beef,
   snipped
3 cups milk
¾ cup shredded American
   cheese (3 ounces)
1 tablespoon snipped parsley

In a medium saucepan cook chopped celery and onion in butter or margarine till onion is tender. Blend in flour, salt, and basil. Stir in smoked beef. Add milk all at once. Cook and stir till thickened and bubbly. Stir in the shredded cheese till melted. Stir in parsley; heat through. Garnish with additional snipped parsley, if desired. Makes 3 or 4 servings.

Beefy Bean Soup
Smoky Beef Chowder

Reuben Chowder

3 cups milk
1 10¾-ounce can condensed
   cream of celery soup
½ cup shredded process Swiss
   cheese (2 ounces)
1 16-ounce can sauerkraut,
   drained and snipped
● ● ●
3 tablespoons butter *or*
   margarine, softened
4 to 6 slices rye bread
1 teaspoon caraway seed
● ● ●
1 12-ounce can corned beef,
   chilled and diced

In a saucepan stir milk into the celery soup and shredded cheese. Add snipped sauerkraut; cover and simmer for 15 minutes.

Meanwhile, spread the butter or margarine over both sides of the rye bread; sprinkle both sides with caraway seed. Cut bread slices into triangles; place on baking sheet. Toast in 300° oven for 20 minutes.

Add diced corned beef to soup. Heat about 10 minutes or till heated through. Serve toast triangles with soup. Makes 4 to 6 servings.

Beefy Bean Soup

3 cups coarsely chopped
   cabbage
1 medium onion, chopped
   (½ cup)
2 cups water
1 17-ounce can lima beans
1 11½-ounce can condensed
   bean with bacon soup
1 tablespoon prepared
   mustard
1 12-ounce can corned beef,
   chilled and diced

In saucepan simmer cabbage and onion in the water, covered, for 8 to 10 minutes or till tender. Stir in the *undrained* beans, soup, and mustard. Stir in corned beef; heat through. Serves 4 to 6.

Ham and Pea Soup

2 11¼-ounce cans condensed
   green pea soup
1 cup chicken broth (see tip,
   page 87)
2 cups milk
1 6¾-ounce can chunk-style
   ham, drained and diced,
   or 1 cup diced fully
   cooked ham
1 2-ounce can mushroom
   stems and pieces
¼ cup dry white wine

In saucepan combine pea soup and chicken broth; stir in milk. Cook and stir till heated through. Stir in ham, *undrained* mushrooms, and wine; heat through. Serves 4 to 6.

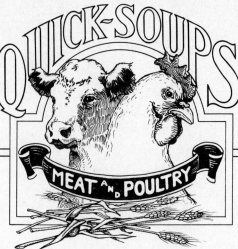

QUICK-SOUPS

MEAT AND POULTRY

Sausage-Vegetable Chowder

This hearty chowder is pictured on page 70 made with lima beans—

2 tablespoons butter *or* margarine
3 tablespoons all-purpose flour
1 teaspoon salt
1 teaspoon onion powder
¼ teaspoon dried dillweed
⅛ teaspoon pepper
4 cups milk
1 10-ounce package frozen vegetable, partially thawed (lima beans, cauliflower, green beans, peas and carrots, *or* broccoli)
1 16-ounce can whole kernel corn, drained
1 12-ounce package smoked sausage links, sliced

In a large saucepan melt butter or margarine over low heat. Blend in flour, salt, onion powder, dillweed, and pepper. Add milk all at once. Cook over medium heat, stirring constantly, till thickened and bubbly.

Cut the partially thawed frozen vegetable into bite-size pieces, if necessary. Stir the vegetable, corn, and sausage into the soup. Cover and simmer for 10 to 15 minutes or till vegetable is done. Makes 6 servings.

Quick and Spicy Sausage Chili

1 8-ounce package brown-and-serve sausage links *or* brown-and-serve sausage patties, cut up
1 small onion, chopped (¼ cup)
½ green pepper, chopped (¼ cup)
1 8-ounce can pork and beans in tomato sauce
1 8-ounce can tomatoes, cut up
¼ cup water
1 tablespoon chili sauce
1 teaspoon chili powder
½ teaspoon sugar
¼ teaspoon salt

In a 2-quart saucepan cook sausage, onion, and green pepper till meat is brown and vegetables are tender. Drain off fat.

Stir in the *undrained* pork and beans, *undrained* tomatoes, water, chili sauce, chili powder, sugar, and salt. Bring mixture to boiling. Reduce heat; cover and simmer for 15 to 20 minutes. Makes 2 or 3 servings.

Bratwurst-Potato Chowder

1 4⅝- or 5½-ounce package dry scalloped potato mix
3 cups water
1 10-ounce package frozen mixed vegetables
3½ cups milk
1 12-ounce package fully cooked smoked bratwurst, sliced, *or* 1 12-ounce can luncheon meat, cubed
½ cup milk
2 tablespoons all-purpose flour

In a Dutch oven or large saucepan combine the potatoes from the scalloped potato mix with the water. Bring to boiling. Reduce heat; cover and simmer for 5 minutes. Add the frozen mixed vegetables. Return to boiling. Reduce heat; cover and simmer for 10 minutes or till potatoes are tender, stirring occasionally. Stir in the 3½ cups milk and the bratwurst or luncheon meat.

Combine the ½ cup milk, the flour, and the seasoning packet from the scalloped potato mix. Stir into the mixture in saucepan. Cook and stir till thickened and bubbly. Cook 2 minutes longer. Makes 6 to 8 servings.

Tomato-Frankfurter Soup

This soup is perfect for the lunch box. Just store it in a widemouthed vacuum container and with it, pack some fresh fruit—

1 large onion, chopped
   (1 cup)
8 ounces frankfurters,
   diagonally sliced
   (4 or 5)
3 tablespoons butter *or*
   margarine
       • • •
1 11½-ounce can condensed
   bean with bacon soup
1 10¾-ounce can condensed
   tomato soup
1½ soup cans water
   (2 cups)
½ teaspoon sugar
½ teaspoon chili powder

In a medium saucepan cook the chopped onion and sliced frankfurters in the butter or margarine till onion is tender but not brown. Stir in bean with bacon soup, tomato soup, water, sugar, and chili powder. Bring to boiling. Reduce heat; cover and simmer for 5 minutes. Makes 3 or 4 servings.

Orange Chicken Stew

Cook the noodles while the vegetables and seasonings simmer—

2 tablespoons butter *or*
   margarine
2 tablespoons all-purpose
   flour
1 8-ounce can tomato sauce
¼ teaspoon finely shredded
   orange peel
⅓ cup orange juice
⅓ cup water
1 8-ounce can sliced
   carrots
1 green pepper, cut into
   ¾-inch squares
   (about 1 cup)
1 tablespoon minced dried
   onion
½ teaspoon sugar
¼ teaspoon salt
¼ teaspoon garlic salt
⅛ teaspoon ground allspice
2 5-ounce cans boned
   chicken, drained and
   cut up
   Hot cooked noodles

In a medium saucepan melt butter or margarine over low heat. Blend in flour. Add tomato sauce, orange peel, orange juice, and water. Cook and stir over medium heat till thickened and bubbly. Stir in *undrained* carrots, green pepper, onion, sugar, salt, garlic salt, and allspice. Bring to boiling. Reduce heat; cover and simmer about 15 minutes. Stir in chicken; heat through. Serve over hot cooked noodles. Makes 3 or 4 servings.

Quick Brunswick Stew

1 large onion, cut in thin
   wedges
1 tablespoon cooking oil
1 16-ounce can stewed
   tomatoes, cut up
1 16-ounce can sliced
   potatoes, drained and
   cut up
1 12-ounce can whole kernel
   corn
1 10¾-ounce can condensed
   tomato soup
1 8-ounce can lima beans,
   drained
½ teaspoon salt
   Dash pepper
2 5-ounce cans boned
   chicken, drained and
   cut up

In a large saucepan cook onion wedges in cooking oil till tender but not brown; stir in *undrained* stewed tomatoes, sliced potatoes, *undrained* whole kernel corn, tomato soup, lima beans, salt, and pepper. Bring mixture to boiling. Reduce heat; cover and simmer mixture for 10 minutes. Carefully stir in the cut-up chicken; continue cooking till heated through. Makes 6 servings.

Peanut-Chicken Soup

¼ cup all-purpose flour
2 teaspoons paprika
1 2½- to 3-pound broiler-
   fryer chicken, cut up
3 tablespoons cooking oil
1 large green pepper,
   chopped (¾ cup)
1 medium onion, chopped
   (½ cup)
3 cups water
3 medium tomatoes, finely
   chopped (1½ cups)
2 teaspoons salt
⅛ teaspoon cayenne
¾ cup creamy peanut butter
2 cups sliced fresh okra or
   1 10-ounce package
   frozen whole okra, sliced
1 4½-ounce can medium
   shrimp, drained and
   deveined

Combine flour and paprika. Coat chicken pieces with flour mixture, using all of the mixture. In large saucepan or Dutch oven brown chicken slowly in hot cooking oil over medium heat about 15 minutes, turning to brown evenly. Remove chicken and set aside. Cook green pepper and onion in pan drippings till tender but not brown. Spoon off excess fat. Add water, tomatoes, salt, cayenne, and chicken pieces to pan. Bring to boiling. Reduce heat; cover and simmer 20 minutes.

In small saucepan heat peanut butter over low heat till melted; gradually blend in about *1 cup* of the hot broth from chicken mixture. Return all to chicken mixture. Stir in okra and shrimp; return to boiling. Reduce heat; cover and simmer 20 minutes or till chicken is tender. Serves 4 to 6.

Chicken Cider Stew

Chicken-Zucchini Stew

Sample this sophisticated, yet inexpensive, chicken entrée—

1½ teaspoons salt
½ teaspoon pepper
¼ teaspoon paprika
1 2½- to 3-pound broiler-
   fryer chicken, cut up
2 tablespoons cooking oil
2 cups chicken broth (see
   tip, page 87)
3 medium potatoes, peeled
   and quartered
1 medium onion, chopped
   (½ cup)
½ teaspoon dried sage,
   crushed
••••
3 medium zucchini, sliced
   (3 cups)
1 4-ounce can mushroom stems
   and pieces, drained
¼ cup dry white wine
3 tablespoons all-purpose
   flour

Combine salt, pepper, and paprika. Rub mixture onto chicken pieces. In large saucepan or Dutch oven brown chicken in hot cooking oil over medium heat about 15 minutes, turning to brown evenly. Add broth, potatoes, onion, and sage. Cover and simmer for 25 minutes.

Stir in zucchini and mushrooms. Simmer about 10 minutes more or till vegetables are tender. Remove chicken and vegetables to serving dish; cover and keep warm.

Blend wine and flour; stir into the broth mixture. Cook and stir till thickened and bubbly. Spoon sauce over chicken and vegetables in serving dish. Makes 4 servings.

Chicken Cider Stew

2 cups apple cider or juice
3 tablespoons catsup
2 slices bacon, cut up
1½ teaspoons salt
¼ teaspoon dried savory,
   crushed
¼ teaspoon dried basil,
   crushed
⅛ teaspoon pepper
1 2- to 2½-pound broiler-
   fryer chicken or rabbit,
   cut up
4 carrots, thinly sliced
2 medium sweet potatoes,
   peeled and quartered
2 medium onions, finely
   chopped (1 cup)
1 stalk celery, cut into
   1-inch pieces
1 apple, peeled, cored, and
   chopped (1 cup)
3 tablespoons all-purpose
   flour

In large kettle or Dutch oven stir together first 7 ingredients. Add chicken or rabbit. Bring to boiling. Reduce heat; cover and simmer for 45 minutes. Stir in carrots, sweet potatoes, onions, celery, and apple. Cover and simmer about 30 minutes or till meat and vegetables are tender. Blend the flour and ¼ cup cold *water;* stir into hot stew. Cook and stir till mixture is thickened and bubbly. Makes 4 servings.

Crockery cooking directions: Use ingredients as listed above. Place carrots, sweet potatoes, onions, celery, and apple in electric slow crockery cooker. Add chicken or rabbit. Combine *1½ cups* of the apple cider, the catsup, bacon, salt, savory, basil, and pepper. Pour over meat and vegetables. Cover and cook on low-heat setting for 10 to 12 hours. Turn cooker to high-heat setting. Blend the flour with the remaining ½ cup cider; stir into hot stew. Cover and cook 15 minutes or till thickened and bubbly.

✦✦ SAUSAGE ✦✦

Beef and Sausage Stew

Beef stew with the added flavor of bacon, Polish sausage, cabbage, and apple—

4 slices bacon
1 pound beef stew meat, cut into 1-inch cubes
3 medium apples, peeled, cored, and chopped (2¾ cups)
1 large onion, chopped (1 cup)
3½ cups beef broth (see tip, page 87)
1 teaspoon salt
• • •
1 pound Polish sausage links, cut into bite-size pieces
6 medium carrots, sliced (3 cups)
6 cups chopped cabbage
¼ cup all-purpose flour

In 4½-quart Dutch oven cook bacon till crisp. Drain, reserving drippings in pan. Crumble bacon and set aside. Brown stew meat in the reserved drippings. Add apples and onion. Cover and simmer for 5 minutes. Add *3 cups* of the beef broth to pot; stir in salt. Bring to boiling. Reduce heat; cover and simmer about 1¼ hours or till meat is nearly tender.

Stir in sausage pieces and carrots. Cover and simmer for 30 minutes. Stir in cabbage; cover and simmer 10 minutes more. Blend the remaining ½ cup beef broth and flour. Stir into stew. Cook and stir till thickened and bubbly. Top each serving with some crumbled bacon. Makes 8 servings.

Sausage Soup

2 slices bacon
1 pound bulk pork sausage
1 medium onion, sliced
3½ cups beef broth (see tip, page 87)
1 8-ounce can *each* French-style green beans, cut wax beans, *and* butter beans, drained
½ teaspoon worcestershire sauce
⅛ teaspoon dry mustard

In skillet cook bacon till crisp. Drain, reserving drippings. Crumble bacon; set aside. Cook sausage and onion in bacon drippings till meat is brown and onion is tender. Remove sausage and onion from skillet; drain on paper toweling. In saucepan combine sausage, onion, broth, the 3 kinds of drained beans, worcestershire, mustard, ¼ teaspoon *salt,* and dash *pepper.* Heat through, stirring occasionally. Top each serving with bacon. Serves 4.

Dutch Pea Soup

1 pound bulk pork sausage
1 pound dry split peas
7 cups water
2 fresh pigs' feet (1¼ pounds)
1 cup finely chopped onion
1 large potato, peeled and shredded (1 cup)
2 teaspoons salt

Shape sausage into ¾-inch balls; brown on all sides in Dutch oven. Drain, reserving 2 tablespoons fat in pan. Rinse peas; add to pan. Stir in remaining ingredients. Bring to boiling; cover and simmer for 1½ hours. Remove pigs' feet; cut off any meat and return to soup. Discard bones. Heat soup; season to taste. Makes 8 to 10 servings.

Chorizo-Garbanzo Stew

If you like, you can freeze part of this Mexican-style stew to serve another time—

1 pound dry garbanzo beans (2½ cups)
13 cups water
1 pound beef shank crosscuts
1 pound smoked pork hocks (ham hocks)
1 large onion, chopped (1 cup)
2 teaspoons salt
2 teaspoons paprika
1 pound chorizo *or* Italian sausage links, sliced
2 medium potatoes, peeled and diced (2 cups)
4 slices bacon, crisp-cooked, drained, and crumbled

Rinse beans. In 10-quart kettle or Dutch oven combine beans and the water. Bring to boiling; reduce heat and simmer 2 minutes. Remove from heat. Cover; let stand 1 hour. (Or, soak beans in the water overnight in a covered pan.) *Do not drain.*

Add beef shank crosscuts, smoked pork hocks, chopped onion, salt, and paprika. Cover and simmer for 2 hours or till beans are tender. Remove meats. Skim fat from soup. When meats have cooled slightly, remove meat from bones and dice. Discard bones.

Return meat to soup. Stir in sausage pieces and potatoes. Bring to boiling. Reduce heat; cover and simmer 20 minutes longer or till potatoes are tender. Sprinkle each serving with some crumbled bacon. Makes 16 servings.

Oven Potato Sausage-Lentil Stew

8 ounces dry lentils
   (1¼ cups)
1½ pounds potato sausage *or*
   Polish sausage, cut into
   ½-inch pieces
2 medium carrots, chopped
   (1 cup)
3 cups water
   ● ● ●
1 stalk celery, chopped
   (½ cup)
1 medium onion, chopped
   (½ cup)
2 tablespoons butter *or*
   margarine
2 tablespoons all-purpose
   flour
1 cup water
½ cup dry red wine
2 teaspoons instant chicken
   bouillon granules
¾ teaspoon dried thyme,
   crushed
¾ teaspoon salt
⅛ teaspoon pepper

Rinse lentils; in saucepan combine with potato sausage or Polish sausage, and carrots. Add the 3 cups water; bring to boiling. Reduce heat; cover and simmer for 30 minutes.

In skillet cook chopped celery and onion in butter or margarine till tender but not brown. Blend in flour; stir in the 1 cup water, the wine, chicken bouillon granules, thyme, salt, and pepper. Bring to boiling, stirring constantly.

In a 2½-quart casserole combine the lentil-sausage mixture with the wine mixture. Bake, uncovered, in 375° oven for 40 minutes, stirring once or twice. Makes 6 servings.

German Sausage Chowder

1 pound fully cooked smoked
   bratwurst *or* knackwurst
   links, cut into ½-inch
   pieces (8 links)
2 medium potatoes, peeled
   and chopped (2 cups)
1 medium onion, chopped
   (½ cup)
1½ teaspoons salt
   Dash pepper
2 cups water
1 small head cabbage,
   shredded (4 cups)
3 cups milk
3 tablespoons all-purpose
   flour
1 cup shredded Swiss cheese
   (4 ounces)
   Snipped parsley

In large saucepan or Dutch oven combine sausage, potatoes, onion, salt, and pepper. Add water. Bring to boiling. Reduce heat; cover and simmer 20 minutes or till potatoes are nearly tender. Stir in cabbage; cook 10 minutes more or till vegetables are tender. Stir in 2½ *cups* of the milk. Blend remaining ½ cup milk and flour; stir into soup. Cook and stir till thickened and bubbly. Stir in cheese till melted. Garnish with parsley. Makes 6 servings.

Sausage Substitutions

Vary the flavor of a soup by using a different sausage with similar qualities. Try Italian sausage or chorizo instead of bulk pork sausage. Or, substitute beerwurst, Polish sausage, or smoked bratwurst for frankfurters. And when a recipe calls for pepperoni, experiment with hard salami or summer sausage.

Beerwurst Soup

2 stalks celery, chopped
   (1 cup)
1 medium onion, chopped
   (½ cup)
2 tablespoons butter *or*
   margarine
1 tablespoon cornstarch
½ teaspoon dry mustard
¼ teaspoon dried oregano,
   crushed
¼ teaspoon dried basil,
   crushed
¼ teaspoon dried thyme,
   crushed
¼ teaspoon garlic powder
1 13¾-ounce can (1¾
   cups) beef broth
1 12-ounce can (1½ cups)
   beer
¾ pound beerwurst (beer
   salami), thinly sliced
   and quartered
   ● ● ●
4 slices French bread cut
   1 inch thick
1 cup shredded mozzarella
   cheese (4 ounces)

In large skillet cook the chopped celery and onion in butter or margarine till tender but not brown. Blend in cornstarch, dry mustard, oregano, basil, thyme, and garlic powder. Add beef broth and beer. Cook and stir till thickened and bubbly. Cover and simmer over low heat for 30 minutes, stirring occasionally. Add beerwurst; simmer 2 to 3 minutes to heat through.

Place bread slices on baking sheet; sprinkle with the shredded mozzarella cheese. Broil 3 inches from heat for 3 minutes or till cheese is melted and lightly browned. Ladle soup into 4 bowls; top each with a bread slice. Makes 4 servings.

Veal-Mushroom Oven-Style Burgoo

Burgoo is another name for a meat and vegetable stew. This mustard and tomato-flavored version is shown on page 60—

- 2 pounds boneless veal, cut into 1-inch cubes
- 2 tablespoons cooking oil
- ¼ cup all-purpose flour
- 2 tablespoons prepared mustard
- 2 teaspoons instant beef bouillon granules
- 1½ teaspoons salt
- 1 teaspoon sugar
- 1 18-ounce can (2¼ cups) tomato juice
- 1 cup water
- 6 small carrots
- 12 whole pearl onions *or* frozen small whole onions
- 2 cups sliced fresh mushrooms (5 ounces)

In large skillet brown meat, *half* at a time, in hot oil. Remove meat to a 3-quart casserole, leaving meat juices in skillet. Stir flour, mustard, bouillon granules, salt, and sugar into meat juices in skillet. Add tomato juice and water; cook and stir till thickened and bubbly. Pour over meat in casserole. Cover and bake in 350° oven for 1 hour.

Cut carrots in half crosswise and then into quarters lengthwise to form thin sticks. Stir carrots, onions, and mushrooms into stew. Cover and bake for 45 to 60 minutes more or till meat and vegetables are tender. Stir before serving. Makes 6 servings.

French Veal Stew

- ¼ cup all-purpose flour
- 1 teaspoon salt
- ¼ teaspoon pepper
- 2 pounds boneless veal, cut into ¾-inch cubes
- ¼ cup cooking oil
- 6 medium carrots, cut into ½-inch pieces
- 1 large onion, quartered
- 1 stalk celery, halved
- 3 sprigs parsley
- 2 cloves garlic, minced
- 1 bay leaf
- ½ teaspoon salt
- ½ teaspoon dried thyme, crushed
- ½ teaspoon dried basil, crushed
- 2 cups water
- ½ cup dry sherry

• • •

- 3 egg yolks
- 1 tablespoon lemon juice
- 1 tablespoon milk
  Hot cooked noodles (optional)

In paper or plastic bag combine flour, the 1 teaspoon salt, and the pepper. Add veal cubes, a few at a time, shaking to coat. In large skillet brown veal cubes, *half* at a time, in hot oil. Return all veal to skillet. Add carrots, onion, celery, parsley, garlic, bay leaf, the ½ teaspoon salt, thyme, and basil. Stir in water and sherry. Bring to boiling. Reduce heat; cover and simmer about 1 hour or till meat is tender. Discard celery, parsley, and bay leaf.

In a bowl beat together egg yolks, lemon juice, and milk. Stir about *1 cup* of the hot mixture into egg yolk mixture; return to remaining hot mixture, stirring constantly. Heat through, stirring constantly. Serve over noodles, if desired. Makes 6 to 8 servings.

Blanquette de Veau

- 3 cups sliced fresh mushrooms, (8 ounces)
- 2 tablespoons butter *or* margarine
- 3 pounds boneless veal, cut into 1-inch cubes
- 2 cloves garlic, minced
- 1 pound small whole onions (about 16)
- 1 cup light cream
- ⅓ cup all-purpose flour
- 1 teaspoon instant chicken bouillon granules
- 1 teaspoon salt
- ⅛ teaspoon white pepper
- ¼ cup dry sherry
- ¼ cup snipped parsley
  Hot cooked noodles (optional)

In large skillet cook mushrooms in butter or margarine till tender. Remove mushrooms to a 3-quart casserole. In same skillet over medium-low heat, cook veal and garlic, covered, for 15 minutes, stirring frequently. Do not allow meat to brown.

Meanwhile, cook onions in boiling salted water for 10 minutes; drain. Add meat and onions to casserole. Measure pan juices; add enough water to make 1 cup liquid. Return liquid to skillet. Blend together light cream and flour. Add to pan juices. Stir in bouillon granules, salt, and pepper. Cook and stir till mixture is thickened and bubbly. Pour over meat and onions in casserole.

Bake in 350° oven about 1 hour or till meat is tender. Stir in sherry. Sprinkle with parsley. Serve with hot cooked noodles, if desired. Makes 8 to 10 servings.

Venison Stew

1 pound boneless venison *or*
  beef stew meat cut into
  ½-inch cubes
1½ cups water
1 teaspoon salt
⅛ teaspoon coarsely ground
  pepper
½ cup dry red wine
4 medium carrots, cut into
  thirds
2 medium potatoes, peeled
  and cubed (2 cups)
1 cup fresh *or* frozen
  cranberries
1 medium onion, chopped
  (½ cup)
1 stalk celery, cut into
  julienne strips
1 clove garlic, minced
2 tablespoons sugar
2 tablespoons worcestershire
  sauce
1½ teaspoons Hungarian *or*
  regular paprika
3 juniper berries (optional)
2 whole cloves
1 bay leaf
½ cup cold water
¼ cup rye flour
  Cooked wild rice *or* sliced
  French bread

In 3-quart saucepan combine venison or beef stew meat with the 1½
cups water, salt, and pepper. Bring to
boiling. Reduce heat; cover and
simmer 1¼ hours. Stir in wine, carrots, potatoes, cranberries, onion,
celery, garlic, sugar, worcestershire
sauce, paprika, juniper berries,
cloves, and bay leaf. Cover and simmer for 45 minutes or till vegetables
are tender. Combine the ½ cup cold
water and rye flour; stir into stew.
Cook and stir till thickened and bubbly. Remove bay leaf. Serve stew
with wild rice or sliced French bread.
Makes 4 servings.

Irish Stew

1 pound boneless lamb, cut
  into 1-inch cubes
1 medium onion, cut into
  thin wedges
1 bay leaf
1½ teaspoons salt
¼ teaspoon pepper
● ● ●
2 medium potatoes, peeled
  and thinly sliced
  (2 cups)
1 medium turnip, peeled and
  chopped (1 cup)
1 9-ounce package frozen
  cut green beans
1 tablespoon snipped parsley
¼ teaspoon dried basil,
  crushed
¼ teaspoon dried oregano,
  crushed

In large saucepan or Dutch oven
combine lamb, onion, bay leaf, salt,
and pepper. Add 4 cups *water.* Bring
to boiling. Reduce heat; cover and
simmer for 1 hour. Stir in potatoes,
turnip, green beans, parsley, basil,
and oregano. Cover and cook 25 to
30 minutes more or till vegetables are
tender. Remove bay leaf. Season to
taste. Makes 6 servings.

Crockery cooking directions: Use
ingredients as listed above. In electric
slow crockery cooker combine onion, bay leaf, salt, pepper, potatoes,
turnip, green beans, parsley, basil,
and oregano. Add lamb cubes; pour
2½ cups *water* over all. Cover and
cook on low-heat setting for 10 to 12
hours. Remove bay leaf. Season to
taste.

Lamb Paprikash

2 pounds lean boneless lamb,
  cut into 1-inch pieces
2 tablespoons cooking oil
1 clove garlic, minced
1 16-ounce can tomatoes,
  cut up
1 large onion, chopped
  (1 cup)
2 teaspoons salt
1 to 2 teaspoons paprika
½ cup cold water
3 tablespoons all-purpose
  flour
1 cup dairy sour cream
  Hot cooked noodles
  Snipped parsley

In large skillet brown *half* the lamb in
hot oil; set aside. Brown remaining
lamb and garlic; return all to skillet.
Stir in *undrained* tomatoes, onion,
salt, and paprika. Bring to boiling.
Reduce heat; cover and simmer 1 to
1½ hours or till meat is tender. Blend
water and flour; stir into stew. Cook
and stir till thickened and bubbly. Stir
about ½ *cup* of the hot gravy into
sour cream. Return to stew. Heat
through but *do not boil.* Serve over
hot noodles. Sprinkle with parsley.
Makes 6 servings.

Crockery cooking directions: Use
ingredients as listed above *except*
omit the cooking oil. In electric slow
crockery cooker combine lamb, garlic, *undrained* tomatoes, onion, salt,
and paprika. Cover and cook on
low-heat setting 8 to 10 hours.

Turn cooker to high-heat setting;
spoon off any fat. Blend cold water
and flour; stir into meat mixture.
Cover; cook 20 to 30 minutes or till
thickened and bubbly. Stir mixture
occasionally. Blend about ½ *cup* of
the hot mixture into sour cream; return to stew in cooker. Heat through.
Serve over hot cooked noodles;
sprinkle with parsley.

Mashed potato mounds circle *SHAKER BEEF GOULASH (left rear)*. This appealing stew is sure to become a family favorite. See recipe on page 34.

Pea pods add an Oriental touch to *SWEET-SOUR PORK STEW (left front)*. See recipe on page 64.

Easy yet company-special *VEAL-MUSHROOM OVEN-STYLE BURGOO (right rear)* simmers in the oven while you greet your guests. See recipe on page 58.

Lamb is enhanced by dill, peas, sour cream, and wine in *DILLED LAMB RAGOUT (right front)*. See recipe on page 62.

Dilled Lamb Ragout

*Garnish stew with lemon wedges and
fresh dill, as shown on page 60—*

2 pounds boneless lamb, cut
　　into ¾-inch cubes
⅓ cup all-purpose flour
½ teaspoon dried dillweed
¼ cup cooking oil
1 10-ounce package (2 cups)
　　frozen peas
1 cup sliced celery
½ cup rosé wine
1 cup dairy sour cream

Coat lamb with mixture of flour,
dillweed, 1½ teaspoons *salt*, and
dash *pepper*. In Dutch oven brown
lamb, *half* at a time, in hot oil. Return
all meat to pan. Stir in any remaining
flour mixture. Blend in 2 cups *water*.
Bake, covered, in 375° oven 45 minutes. Stir in peas, celery, and wine;
cover and bake 45 minutes more.
Skim off fat. Stir in sour cream. Heat
through but *do not boil*. Serves 6.

Ham Hodgepodge

5 cups chopped cabbage
6 large carrots, cut into
　　1-inch pieces (1 pound)
2 large potatoes, peeled and
　　chopped (3 cups)
2 cups diced fully cooked
　　ham (10 ounces)
½ cup chopped onion
½ teaspoon seasoned salt
1 15-ounce can garbanzo
　　beans

In Dutch oven combine first 6 ingredients, 3 cups *water*, ½ teaspoon *salt*,
and ⅛ teaspoon *pepper*. Cover; simmer 1 hour. Add *undrained* beans;
cover and cook 10 to 15 minutes.
(Add more water, if needed.) Makes
6 to 8 servings.

Lamb and Lentil Soup

*This meaty soup made with lamb
shanks, a ham hock, and knackwurst
tastes like a French cassoulet—*

4 lamb shanks (about 3
　　pounds)
1 medium smoked pork hock
　　(ham hock)
1 medium onion, chopped
　　(½ cup)
1 clove garlic, halved
1½ teaspoons salt
¼ teaspoon pepper
8 cups water
　　• • •
1½ cups dry lentils
2 knackwurst links, sliced
　　(about 6 ounces)
2 medium carrots, chopped
　　(1 cup)
1 cup dry red wine
3 tablespoons snipped
　　parsley
½ teaspoon dried thyme,
　　crushed
¼ teaspoon dried rosemary,
　　crushed

In very large kettle combine lamb
shanks, pork hock, onion, garlic, salt,
and pepper. Add the water; bring to
boiling. Reduce heat; cover and
simmer for 2 hours.
　　Remove lamb shanks and pork
hock. When meats are cool enough
to handle, cut off meat and chop. Return chopped meat to broth; discard
bones.
　　Rinse lentils; add to soup. Stir in
sliced knackwurst, carrots, wine,
parsley, thyme, and rosemary. Cover
and simmer mixture 45 to 50 minutes
or till lentils and carrots are tender.
Skim off fat. Season to taste with
salt and pepper. Makes 8 servings.

Ham-Spinach Chowder

1 10-ounce package frozen
　　chopped spinach
½ cup chopped onion
1 10¾-ounce can condensed
　　cream of potato soup
3½ cups milk
3 cups cubed fully cooked
　　ham (1 pound)
¼ cup snipped parsley
2 teaspoons prepared mustard
¾ teaspoon salt
½ teaspoon dried basil,
　　crushed
　　Dash pepper
3 tablespoons all-purpose
　　flour

In large saucepan cook frozen spinach and onion according to spinach
package directions; drain well. Blend
potato soup into spinach. Stir in *3
cups* of the milk, the ham, parsley,
mustard, salt, basil, and pepper.
Cook over low heat till heated
through; stir occasionally.
　　Blend the remaining ½ cup milk
and the flour; stir into ham mixture.
Cook and stir till thickened and bubbly. If desired, dot each serving with
butter or margarine. Serves 6.
　　Microwave cooking directions: In
2-quart nonmetal casserole place frozen spinach and onion. Cook,
covered with waxed paper, in countertop microwave oven on high
power for 5 to 7 minutes or till vegetables are tender, stirring and breaking up spinach once. Drain. Blend
potato soup into spinach mixture.
Stir in *3 cups* of the milk, the ham,
parsley, mustard, salt, basil, and pepper. Micro-cook, covered, about 5
minutes or till heated through, stirring
once. Blend the remaining ½ cup
milk and flour; stir into ham mixture.
Micro-cook, uncovered, for 8 to 10
minutes or till slightly thickened and
bubbly, stirring every 2 minutes.
Serve as above.

Hot and Hearty Ham Soup

Cheese-topped rye bread slices float atop individual servings of soup as shown on page 44—

1 1½- to 1¾-pound meaty ham bone *or* 1½ pounds smoked pork hocks (ham hocks)
8 cups water
8 whole black peppercorns
5 whole cloves
1 teaspoon salt
1 clove garlic, halved
3½ cups coarsely chopped cabbage
2 large potatoes, peeled and thinly sliced (3 cups)
3 large carrots, thinly sliced (2 cups)
1 medium onion, chopped (½ cup)
6 to 8 thick slices rye bread
¼ cup grated parmesan cheese
4 ounces Swiss cheese, cut into strips

In 4½-quart Dutch oven combine ham bone or hocks, water, peppercorns, cloves, salt, and garlic; bring to boiling. Reduce heat; cover and simmer 2½ hours. Remove ham bone; when bone is cool enough to handle, cut off meat and chop. Discard bone. Strain broth. Return broth and meat to Dutch oven. Add cabbage, potatoes, carrots, and onion. Cover and simmer 40 minutes or till vegetables are tender. Season to taste with salt and pepper.

Meanwhile, toast bread. Ladle soup into heat-proof bowls. Top each with a toast slice; sprinkle with parmesan and top with Swiss cheese. Place under broiler 2 minutes or till cheese melts. (Or, if you don't have heat-proof bowls, place toast slices on baking sheet; top with cheese, and broil. Float atop soup servings.) Makes 6 to 8 servings.

Broccoli and Ham Soup

2 cups diced fully cooked ham (10 ounces)
1 medium onion, chopped (½ cup)
1 clove garlic, minced
2 tablespoons butter *or* margarine
2 10¾-ounce cans *condensed* chicken broth
2 cups chopped fresh broccoli *or* 1 10-ounce package frozen chopped broccoli
1½ cups water
1 8-ounce can tomatoes, cut up
½ cup elbow macaroni
¼ teaspoon ground nutmeg
Grated parmesan cheese (optional)

In 3-quart saucepan cook ham, onion, and garlic in butter or margarine till onion is tender. Stir in condensed chicken broth, fresh or frozen chopped broccoli, water, *undrained* tomatoes, uncooked macaroni, and nutmeg. Bring to boiling. Reduce heat; cover and simmer for 8 to 10 minutes or till broccoli and macaroni are tender. Season to taste with some salt and pepper. Sprinkle individual servings with parmesan cheese, if desired. Makes 6 servings.

Cutting Tomatoes

When a recipe calls for cut-up canned tomatoes, do the cutting in the can. Insert a sharp knife into the open can and cut tomatoes against the side of the can. Or, use kitchen shears to snip the tomatoes. Draining is usually unnecessary, since you'll also use the liquid.

Schnitz Und Knepp

If you buy home-style dried apples you'll need to add them earlier—

1 2- to 2½-pound smoked pork shoulder roll
4 cups chicken broth (see tip, page 87)
2 cups water
8 ounces dried apples (2 cups)
2 tablespoons brown sugar
Potato Dumplings *or* Fluffy Dumplings (see recipe, page 90)

Trim excess fat from pork. Place pork in 4½-quart Dutch oven; add broth and water. Bring to boiling; cover and simmer 1½ to 2 hours or till pork is tender. Turn meat occasionally during cooking. Skim fat from broth. Remove meat; cut into bite-size pieces. Return meat to Dutch oven. Add apples and sugar. Bring to boiling, stirring to dissolve sugar.

Prepare Potato or Fluffy Dumplings. Drop dough from tablespoon into 8 mounds atop bubbling broth. Cover tightly and let mixture return to boiling. Reduce heat (don't lift cover); simmer 30 minutes for Potato Dumplings or 15 minutes for Fluffy Dumplings. (Potato Dumplings will be soft.) To serve, remove dumplings to serving bowl with slotted spoon; pour meat and apple mixture around dumplings. Makes 8 servings.

Potato Dumplings: In saucepan barely cover 4 medium *potatoes* (1¼ pounds) with water. Add 1 teaspoon *salt*. Bring to boiling. Reduce heat; cover and simmer for 20 minutes or till potatoes are tender. Drain and cool slightly. Peel potatoes. Mash with 2 tablespoons *butter or margarine* and ½ teaspoon *salt* till very smooth. Stir in ¼ cup all-purpose *flour* and 2 beaten *eggs*; mix well.

Sweet-Sour Pork Stew

Use fresh or frozen pea pods to make this stew, shown on page 60—

¼ cup all-purpose flour
1 teaspoon salt
  Dash pepper
2 pounds boneless pork, cut into ¾-inch cubes
2 tablespoons cooking oil
1½ cups chicken broth (see tip, page 87)
⅓ cup catsup
2 tablespoons vinegar
1 tablespoon brown sugar
1 teaspoon salt
1 teaspoon worcestershire sauce
1 large onion, chopped (1 cup)
4 cups fresh pea pods *or* 2 6-ounce packages frozen pea pods partially thawed
  Hot cooked rice *or* hot cooked noodles

In paper or plastic bag combine flour, 1 teaspoon salt, and the pepper. Add pork cubes, a few at a time, shaking to coat. In large saucepan or Dutch oven brown meat, *half* at a time, in hot oil. Return all meat to saucepan.

Combine chicken broth, catsup, vinegar, brown sugar, 1 teaspoon salt, and worcestershire sauce. Stir into meat; add onion, Cover and simmer about 1 hour or till meat is tender, stirring occasionally. Stir in fresh or frozen pea pods; cover and simmer 3 to 5 minutes longer or till pea pods are crisp-tender. Serve with rice or noodles. Makes 6 to 8 servings.

Pork Brunswick Stew

Serve with seasoned croutons for added flavor and texture—

¾ cup soft bread crumbs (1 slice)
¼ cup milk
¾ teaspoon salt
¾ teaspoon ground sage
1 pound ground pork
2 tablespoons cooking oil
1 28-ounce can tomatoes, cut up
1 16-ounce can whole kernel corn
1 medium onion, chopped (½ cup)
1 tablespoon vinegar
1 tablespoon prepared mustard
2 teaspoons sugar
1½ teaspoons salt
½ teaspoon worcestershire sauce

Combine crumbs, milk, the ¾ teaspoon salt, and sage. Add pork; mix well. Shape into 36 one-inch balls. In Dutch oven brown meatballs, *half* at a time, in hot oil. Drain off fat. Return all meatballs to Dutch oven; stir in remaining ingredients. Bring to boiling. Reduce heat; cover and simmer 30 minutes. Makes 4 to 6 servings.

Microwave cooking directions: Use ingredients as listed above *except* omit cooking oil. Mix and shape meatballs as directed above.

Arrange meatballs in a 12x7½x2-inch nonmetal baking dish. Cook, covered with waxed paper, in countertop microwave oven on high power about 6 minutes or till meat is done; rearrange twice. Drain and set aside.

In 3-quart nonmetal casserole combine remaining ingredients, omitting oil. Micro-cook, covered, 11 to 12 minutes or till heated through, stirring twice. Stir in meatballs. Micro-cook, uncovered, 1 minute more.

Pork and Cabbage Soup

This meal-in-a-dish soup combines shredded cabbage and pork cubes in a beef-tomato broth. It's pictured on page 44—

1 pound lean boneless pork, cut into ½-inch cubes
1 tablespoon cooking oil
1 10¾-ounce can condensed tomato soup
1 10½-ounce can *condensed* beef broth
2 soup cans water (2½ cups)
1 small head cabbage, shredded (4 cups)
1 medium onion, chopped (½ cup)
¼ cup dry sherry
1 bay leaf
1 teaspoon salt
½ teaspoon paprika
  Dash pepper
• • •
  Dairy sour cream

In 4½-quart Dutch oven brown pork cubes in hot cooking oil. Drain off excess fat. Stir in tomato soup, condensed beef broth, water, shredded cabbage, chopped onion, sherry, bay leaf, salt, paprika, and pepper. Bring mixture to boiling. Reduce heat; cover and simmer 40 minutes or till meat is tender. Remove bay leaf. Season to taste with additional salt and pepper. Top each serving with a dollop of sour cream. Garnish with a parsley sprig, if desired. Makes 5 or 6 servings.

South American Pork Soup

This soup can be made in an electric slow crockery cooker or a Dutch oven. It's pictured on page 36—

1½ pounds lean boneless pork *or* beef, cut into ½-inch cubes
2 tablespoons cooking oil
1 medium onion, finely chopped (½ cup)
1 clove garlic, minced
1 teaspoon paprika
2 medium potatoes, peeled and cut into ½-inch cubes (2 cups)
2 medium sweet potatoes, peeled and cut into ½-inch cubes (2 cups)
2 medium carrots, chopped (1 cup)
½ small winter squash, peeled and cut into ½-inch cubes (1 cup)
1 8-ounce can whole kernel corn
1 tomato, peeled and chopped
2 teaspoons salt
¼ teaspoon pepper
2 cups torn fresh spinach

In 4-quart Dutch oven or kettle brown *half* the meat in hot oil; remove from pan. Brown remaining meat with onion, garlic, and paprika. Return all meat to pan. Add 3 cups *water.* Bring to boiling. Reduce heat; cover and simmer 1¼ hours. Add potatoes, sweet potatoes, carrots, squash, *undrained* corn, tomato, salt, and pepper. Cover; simmer 15 to 20 minutes more or till meat and vegetables are tender. Stir in spinach; simmer 3 to 5 minutes more. Season to taste with salt and pepper. Makes 8 servings.

Crockery cooking directions: Use ingredients as listed above. In large skillet brown *half* the meat in hot oil; set aside. Brown remaining meat with onion, garlic, and paprika. In electric slow crockery cooker arrange potatoes, sweet potatoes, carrots, squash, *undrained* corn, tomato, salt, and pepper. Place meat and onion mixture atop vegetables; pour 2½ cups *water* over all. Cover and cook on low-heat setting for 8 hours or till meat and vegetables are tender. Turn to high-heat setting. Stir in spinach. Cover and cook 10 minutes or till spinach is slightly wilted. Season to taste.

Fresh Cauliflower-Ham Chowder

This creamy chowder is also easy to make. It's shown on page 70—

2 medium potatoes, peeled and cubed (2 cups)
1 cup water
1 medium onion, chopped (½ cup)
1 tablespoon instant chicken bouillon granules
2 cups sliced cauliflowerets
3 cups milk
2½ cups cubed fully cooked ham
⅛ teaspoon ground nutmeg
⅛ teaspoon white pepper
2 tablespoons all-purpose flour
Snipped parsley

In a large saucepan simmer potatoes, water, onion, and bouillon granules, covered, for 10 minutes. Add cauliflower and cook about 10 minutes more or till tender. Stir in *2½ cups* of the milk, the ham, nutmeg, and pepper. Bring to boiling. Blend remaining ½ cup milk with flour. Stir into hot mixture. Cook and stir till thickened and bubbly. Garnish with snipped parsley. Makes 4 to 6 servings.

Barbecue Pork Stew

2 pounds boneless pork, cut into 1-inch cubes
1 to 2 tablespoons cooking oil
1 clove garlic, minced
3 cups water
1 teaspoon salt
¼ teaspoon pepper
• • •
1 small head cabbage, coarsely chopped (4 cups)
1 15-ounce can tomato sauce
1 cup whole pearl onions *or* frozen small whole onions
1 medium green pepper, chopped (½ cup)
½ cup dry red wine
2 tablespoons brown sugar
2 tablespoons prepared mustard
½ teaspoon ground ginger
¼ teaspoon cayenne
Corn Dumplings (see recipe, page 91)

In Dutch oven brown *half* the pork in hot oil. Remove from pan. Brown remaining pork and garlic. Drain off fat. Return all meat to Dutch oven. Add water, salt, and pepper. Bring to boiling. Reduce heat; cover and simmer for 30 minutes. Stir in cabbage, tomato sauce, onions, green pepper, wine, brown sugar, mustard, ginger, and cayenne. Cover and simmer 20 minutes longer or till meat and vegetables are nearly tender. Drop dumplings atop boiling mixture. Cover and simmer 10 to 12 minutes longer or till dumplings are done. Makes 8 servings.

FISH AND SEAFOOD

Seafood Gumbo

½ cup all-purpose flour
½ cup cooking oil
2 medium onions, finely
    chopped (1 cup)
2 stalks celery, finely
    chopped (1 cup)
1 medium green pepper,
    finely chopped (½ cup)
2 cloves garlic, minced
8 cups water
1½ teaspoons salt
½ teaspoon bottled hot
    pepper sauce
1 pound fresh or frozen
    crab meat, thawed
1 pound fresh or frozen
    shelled shrimp
1 pint shucked oysters
¼ cup sliced green
    onion tops
¼ cup snipped parsley
1 tablespoon filé powder
    (optional)
    Hot cooked rice

In Dutch oven or kettle blend together flour and oil. Cook over medium heat 15 minutes or till mixture is a dark reddish-brown color. Stir frequently for the first 10 minutes and stir constantly for the last 5 minutes. Add onions, celery, green pepper, and garlic. Cook and stir about 8 minutes or till vegetables are lightly browned. Add water, salt, and hot pepper sauce. Bring to boiling. Reduce heat; cover and simmer 1 hour.

Add crab meat and shrimp; simmer, uncovered, 15 minutes more. Add oysters and oyster liquid; simmer about 5 minutes more or just till edges of oysters curl. Stir in green onion tops and parsley. Blend a small amount of the hot liquid into filé powder; return all to kettle. Season to taste with salt and pepper. Ladle into bowls over mounds of rice. Makes 8 to 10 servings.

Whiting Stew

2 pounds fresh or frozen
    dressed whiting or other
    fish
2 cups water
⅓ cup snipped parsley
4 cloves garlic
½ teaspoon salt
1 medium onion, sliced
1 stalk celery, sliced
    (½ cup)
2 tablespoons olive or
    cooking oil
2 medium potatoes, peeled
    and sliced
2 large carrots, sliced
    (1 cup)
3 tomatoes, peeled and cubed
1 teaspoon salt
¼ teaspoon pepper

Thaw fish, if frozen. Remove skin from fish. In 10-inch skillet combine fish, water, parsley, garlic, and the ½ teaspoon salt. Bring mixture to boiling. Reduce heat; cover and simmer gently about 2 to 3 minutes or till fish flakes easily when tested with a fork.

In 4-quart Dutch oven cook onion and celery in hot oil till vegetables are tender but not brown. Add potatoes and carrots; cook and stir till lightly browned. Stir in tomatoes, the 1 teaspoon salt, and the pepper.

Strain stock from fish; discard parsley and garlic. Add stock to Dutch oven. Bring to boiling. Reduce heat, cover pan tightly and simmer about 30 minutes or till vegetables are tender.

Meanwhile remove and discard bones from fish; break fish into chunks. Add fish to vegetable mixture; heat through. Makes 6 servings.

Seafood Stew

1 6-ounce package frozen
    crab meat
1 pound fresh or frozen fish
    fillets
8 clams in shells
2 cups Fish Stock (see
    recipe, page 88)
1 16-ounce can tomatoes,
    cut up
¾ cup dry white wine
1 ear fresh corn, cut into
    1-inch pieces or
    1 8-ounce can whole
    kernel corn, drained
½ cup chopped green pepper
1 medium onion, chopped
    (½ cup)
2 tablespoons snipped parsley
1 bay leaf
1 clove garlic, minced
1 teaspoon salt
1 teaspoon dried thyme,
    crushed
¼ teaspoon thread saffron,
    crushed
¼ teaspoon pepper

Partially thaw crab meat and fish. Remove skin from fish fillets; cut fillets into 1-inch pieces. Thoroughly wash clams. Cover clams with salted water using 3 tablespoons salt to 8 cups cold water. Let stand 15 minutes; rinse. Repeat twice.

In large saucepan combine Fish Stock, undrained tomatoes, wine, corn, green pepper, onion, parsley, bay leaf, garlic, salt, thyme, saffron, and pepper. Bring to boiling. Reduce heat; cover and simmer for 30 minutes. Add crab, fish, and clams. Cook 4 to 5 minutes or till fish flakes easily with a fork and clams open. Do not overcook. Discard bay leaf. Serve stew with French bread slices, if desired. Makes 6 to 8 servings.

Seafood Stew

66

Scallop-Wine Soup

1 pound fresh *or* frozen
    scallops, thawed
1 large onion
2 tablespoons butter
¼ cup all-purpose flour
3½ cups milk
1 4-ounce can mushroom
    stems and pieces, drained
½ cup dry white wine
½ cup shredded Swiss cheese
1 tablespoon snipped parsley

Halve large scallops. Cut onion into
thin wedges. Cook onion in butter,
covered, over low heat 15 minutes or
till tender; stir occasionally. Stir in
flour. Add milk; cook and stir over
medium-high heat till bubbly. Add
mushrooms, scallops, 1 teaspoon
salt, and dash *pepper*. Cover; simmer 5 minutes. Stir in wine; heat. Top
with cheese and parsley. Serves 6.

Shrimp Bisque

A creamy soup shown on page 70—

1 cup chopped celery
1 cup diced potato
½ cup chopped onion
2 cups milk
2 tablespoons all-purpose
    flour
1 8-ounce package frozen
    precooked shrimp, thawed
2 tablespoons butter

In saucepan combine celery, potato,
onion, 1 cup *water*, ½ teaspoon *salt*,
and dash *pepper*. Bring to boiling.
Reduce heat; cover and simmer 15
minutes or till potatoes are tender,
stirring occasionally. Blend milk and
flour; stir into potato mixture. Add
shrimp and butter. Cook and stir till
thickened and bubbly. Garnish with
snipped parsley, if desired. Makes 4
servings.

Fish Soup

*This soup, shown on page 36, is
adapted from a Chilean favorite,
Caldillo de Pescado—*

1½ pounds fresh *or* frozen
    fish fillets
1 large onion, chopped
    (1 cup)
1 clove garlic, minced
2 tablespoons olive *or*
    cooking oil
2 cups water
2 small potatoes, peeled and
    diced (1½ cups)
2 tomatoes, peeled and
    diced (1 cup)
½ cup dry white wine
½ teaspoon salt
    Dash pepper
2 beaten egg yolks
2 tablespoons snipped parsley

Thaw fish, if frozen; cut fish into
¾-inch pieces. In large saucepan
cook and stir the chopped onion and
garlic in hot olive or cooking oil till
onion is tender but not brown. Stir in
water, potatoes, tomatoes, wine, salt,
and pepper. Bring to boiling. Reduce
heat; cover and simmer 20 minutes.
Add fish pieces; return to boiling.
Cover and simmer 10 minutes or till
fish flakes easily when tested with a
fork.
    Gradually stir about *1 cup* of the
hot liquid into the beaten egg yolks;
return all to saucepan. Cook and stir
gently till mixture is slightly thickened
and bubbly. Stir in the snipped
parsley. Makes 6 to 8 servings.

Fish-Wine Chowder

1 pound fresh *or* frozen
    brook trout *or* pike
    fillets
1 pound fresh *or* frozen
    halibut *or* haddock
    fillets
6 slices bacon
1 medium onion, chopped
    (½ cup)
2 shallots, chopped
    (1 tablespoon)
1½ cups white burgundy
    or aligote
1½ cups water
1 teaspoon salt
¼ teaspoon dried thyme,
    crushed
1 stalk celery, quartered
2 cloves garlic, halved
4 sprigs parsley
2 whole cloves
3 tablespoons all-purpose
    flour
3 tablespoons butter *or*
    margarine, softened
¼ cup light cream

Thaw fish, if frozen; cut fish into bite-
size pieces. Cook bacon in 4½-quart
Dutch oven; drain, reserving 2 tablespoons drippings. Crumble bacon
and set aside. Cook onion and shallots in reserved bacon drippings till
tender. Remove from heat. Add
wine, water, salt, and thyme. Tie celery, garlic, parsley, and whole cloves
in cheesecloth to make a *bouquet
garni;* add to pan. Bring to boiling.
Reduce heat; cover and simmer for
20 minutes. Remove cheesecloth
bag. Add fish to Dutch oven. Cover
and cook gently about 8 to 10 minutes or till fish flakes when tested with
a fork.
    Blend flour and softened butter or
margarine to a smooth paste; stir into
simmering liquid. Stir in cream. Cook
and stir till thickened and bubbly. Return bacon to pan. Season to taste.
Makes 8 servings.

Fish Goulash

2 medium onions, sliced
1 medium green pepper, cut into rings
2 cloves garlic, minced
3 tablespoons butter or margarine
1 tablespoon paprika
1 15-ounce can tomato sauce
2 cups water
2 teaspoons sugar
1½ teaspoons salt
½ teaspoon dried marjoram, crushed
1½ pounds fresh or frozen haddock, halibut, or salmon steaks, cut ¾ inch thick
10 cherry tomatoes, halved

Thaw fish, if frozen. Cut steaks into 6 serving-size pieces. In 5-quart Dutch oven cook onions, green pepper, and garlic in butter or margarine about 10 minutes or till the vegetables are tender but not brown. Stir in paprika; cook and stir over low heat 2 to 3 minutes. Stir in tomato sauce, water, sugar, salt, and marjoram. Add fish. Bring to boiling. Reduce heat; simmer, uncovered, 15 minutes or till fish flakes easily with a fork. Add tomatoes; cook 5 minutes more. Remove fish to bowls; spoon soup atop. Makes 6 servings.

Fish Terms

A dressed fish is one that's been eviscerated and scaled.
Steaks are crosscut slices from a large, dressed fish. They contain a cross section of the backbone.
Fillets are pieces cut lengthwise from the sides and away from the backbone. They're generally boneless pieces.

Bouillabaisse Gumbo

1 16-ounce can stewed tomatoes
1 10¾-ounce can condensed tomato soup
1 10¾-ounce can condensed chicken gumbo soup
2 soup cans water (2½ cups)
1 medium sweet potato, peeled and chopped (1 cup)
1 stalk celery, chopped (½ cup)
⅓ cup chopped green onion
1 tablespoon snipped parsley
1 tablespoon worcestershire sauce
1 clove garlic, minced
2 dashes bottled hot pepper sauce
1 bay leaf
1 7½-ounce can minced clams
1 4½-ounce can shrimp, drained and deveined
Salt and pepper

In large saucepan combine *undrained* stewed tomatoes, condensed tomato soup, condensed chicken gumbo soup, water, sweet potato, celery, green onion, parsley, worcestershire sauce, garlic, bottled hot pepper sauce, and bay leaf. Bring mixture to boiling. Reduce heat; cover and simmer about 30 minutes or till vegetables are tender. Add *undrained* clams and drained shrimp. Simmer about 10 minutes or till mixture is heated through. Season to taste with salt and pepper. Remove bay leaf before serving. Makes 6 to 8 servings.

Monterey Fish Stew

1 pound fresh or frozen firm, white fish (such as cod, haddock, or sole)
1 small onion, diced (⅓ cup)
1 clove garlic, minced
2 tablespoons butter or margarine
1 cup water
⅓ cup dry vermouth
2 teaspoons instant chicken bouillon granules
¾ teaspoon salt
½ teaspoon dried marjoram, crushed
⅛ teaspoon pepper
1 bay leaf
2 potatoes, peeled and sliced (2 cups)
1 carrot, sliced (½ cup)
2 medium tomatoes, peeled and chopped (1½ cups)
5 or 6 fresh mushrooms, quartered
2 tablespoons snipped parsley
¼ cup cold water
2 tablespoons cornstarch

Thaw fish, if frozen; cut fish into bite-size pieces. In 3-quart saucepan cook onion and garlic in butter or margarine till tender but not brown. Stir in the 1 cup water, the vermouth, bouillon granules, salt, marjoram, pepper, and bay leaf. Add potatoes and carrot; bring to boiling. Reduce heat; cover and simmer about 20 minutes or till vegetables are just tender. Add fish, tomatoes, mushrooms, and parsley. Cover and simmer about 5 minutes or till fish flakes easily with a fork.

Remove fish and vegetables; set aside. Blend the ¼ cup cold water and cornstarch; stir into pan. Cook and stir till thickened and bubbly. Return fish and vegetables to sauce; heat through. Serves 4.

Ladle generous servings of *TUNA-CHEESE CHOWDER (left front)* to please the whole family and stretch the food budget at the same time. See recipe on page 72.

This *SAUSAGE-VEGETABLE CHOWDER (left rear)* goes together in minutes with your choice of vegetables—limas, cauliflower, beans, peas and carrots, or broccoli. See recipe on page 52.

Serve *FRESH CAULIFLOW-ER-HAM CHOWDER (right front)* with chowder crackers, or ones you make yourself. This soup gains body from cooked potatoes. See recipe on page 65.

Frozen shrimp makes *SHRIMP BISQUE (right rear)* a special soup you can proudly serve any time. See recipe on page 68.

Tuna-Cheese Chowder

A terrific family-style soup, shown on page 70—

2 medium carrots, shredded
  (1 cup)
1 medium onion, chopped
  (½ cup)
¼ cup butter *or* margarine
¼ cup all-purpose flour
2 cups milk
2 cups chicken broth
  (see tip, page 87)
1 6½- or 7-ounce can tuna,
  drained and flaked
½ teaspoon celery seed
½ teaspoon worcestershire
  sauce
¼ teaspoon salt
1 cup shredded American
  cheese (4 ounces)
  Snipped chives

In 3-quart saucepan cook carrots and onion in butter or margarine till onion is tender but not brown. Blend in flour. Add milk and chicken broth. Cook and stir till thickened and bubbly. Stir in tuna, celery seed, worcestershire sauce, and salt. Heat through. Add cheese; heat and stir till cheese is melted. Garnish with snipped chives. Makes 4 servings.

Testing Fish for Doneness

The test for doneness of fish is simple. Place fork tines into fish at a 45-degree angle and twist the fork. If the fish flakes apart easily and is milky white, it is done just right. If it resists flaking and still has some translucency, the fish needs additional cooking.

Eggplant-Zucchini Fish Stew

This fish stew is chock-full of interesting vegetables—

2 pounds fresh *or* frozen
  fish fillets
1 medium onion, thinly
  sliced
1 large green pepper,
  chopped (¾ cup)
1 clove garlic, minced
2 tablespoons cooking oil
3 cups tomato juice
1½ teaspoons salt
1 teaspoon sugar
1 teaspoon dried basil,
  crushed
¼ teaspoon pepper
1 medium eggplant, peeled
  and diced (5 cups)
2 medium zucchini, sliced
  (about 2 cups)
  Grated parmesan cheese

Thaw fish, if frozen. Remove skin from fillets and cut fillets into 1-inch pieces; set aside. In 4-quart Dutch oven cook onion, green pepper, and garlic in hot oil till onion is tender but not brown. Stir in tomato juice, salt, sugar, basil, and pepper. Add eggplant; cover and cook about 10 minutes or till eggplant is tender. Stir in zucchini and fish. Cover and cook 10 to 15 minutes longer or till zucchini is tender and fish flakes easily when tested with a fork; stir occasionally. Ladle into soup bowls and sprinkle each serving with some grated parmesan cheese. Serves 6 to 8.

Skip Jack Chowder

1 cup chopped red onion
¼ cup snipped parsley
2 tablespoons butter
1 tablespoon soy sauce
1 teaspoon dried thyme,
  crushed
½ teaspoon salt
1 bay leaf
  Dash bottled hot pepper
  sauce
1 pint shucked oysters
2 cups milk
½ cup light cream
2 cups shredded American
  cheese (8 ounces)
½ cup dry white wine

In saucepan cook onion and parsley in butter till onion is tender. Stir in soy, thyme, salt, bay leaf, and pepper sauce. Add *undrained* oysters; cook and stir over medium heat 5 minutes or till edges of oysters curl. Stir in milk and cream; heat through. Stir in cheese till melted. Remove from heat; stir in wine. Remove bay leaf. Makes 6 servings.

Oyster Stew

1 pint shucked oysters
¾ teaspoon salt
2 cups milk
1 cup light cream
  Dash bottled hot pepper
  sauce (optional)
  Paprika
  Butter *or* margarine

In a medium saucepan combine *undrained* oysters and salt. Cook over medium heat about 5 minutes or till edges of oysters curl. Stir in milk, cream, and hot pepper sauce. Heat through. Season to taste with salt and pepper. Sprinkle each serving with paprika and top with a pat of butter. Makes 4 servings.

Cioppino

This herb-seasoned fish stew is pictured on the cover—

1 pound fresh *or* frozen
   fish fillets
½ large green pepper, cut
   into ½-inch squares
2 tablespoons finely chopped
   onion
1 clove garlic, minced
1 tablespoon cooking oil
1 16-ounce can tomatoes,
   cut up
1 8-ounce can tomato sauce
½ cup dry white *or* red wine
3 tablespoons snipped
   parsley
½ teaspoon salt
¼ teaspoon dried oregano,
   crushed
¼ teaspoon dried basil,
   crushed
   Dash pepper
2 4½-ounce cans shrimp,
   drained and deveined,
   or 1 12-ounce package
   frozen shelled shrimp
1 7½-ounce can minced clams

Thaw fish, if frozen. Remove skin from fillets and cut fillets into 1-inch pieces; set aside.

In 3-quart saucepan cook green pepper, onion, and garlic in oil till onion is tender but not brown. Add *undrained* tomatoes, tomato sauce, wine, parsley, salt, oregano, basil, and pepper. Bring to boiling. Reduce heat; cover and simmer 20 minutes.

Add fish pieces, shrimp, and *undrained* clams to tomato mixture. Bring just to boiling. Reduce heat; cover and simmer 5 to 7 minutes or till fish and shrimp are done. Makes 6 servings.

Bouillabaisse

1 pound small fresh *or*
   frozen lobster tails
1 pound fresh *or* frozen red
   snapper *or* sole fillets
1 pound fresh *or* frozen cod
   or haddock fillets
12 ounces fresh *or* frozen
   scallops
12 clams in shells
2 large onions, chopped
   (2 cups)
⅓ cup olive *or* cooking oil
6 cups Fish Stock (see
   recipe, page 88) *or* water
1 28-ounce can tomatoes,
   cut up
2 small cloves garlic,
   minced
2 sprigs parsley
2 bay leaves
1 tablespoon salt
1½ teaspoons dried thyme,
   crushed
½ teaspoon thread saffron,
   crushed
⅛ teaspoon pepper
   French bread slices

Thaw shellfish and fish, if frozen. When lobster is partially thawed, split tails in half lengthwise; cut crosswise to make 6 to 8 portions. Cut fish fillets into 2-inch pieces. Cut large scallops in half. Wash clams well. Set seafood aside.

In large saucepan or Dutch oven cook onions in hot oil till tender but not brown. Add Fish Stock, *undrained* tomatoes, garlic, parsley, bay leaves, salt, thyme, saffron, and pepper. Bring to boiling. Reduce heat; cover and simmer 30 minutes. Strain stock into a large kettle; discard vegetables and herbs.

Bring strained stock to boiling; add lobster and fish and cook 5 minutes. Add scallops and clams; boil 5 minutes or till clams open. Serve in shallow bowls with French bread. Makes 6 to 8 servings.

Snapper Stew with Lemon Dumplings

1½ pounds fresh *or* frozen red
   snapper *or* other fish
   fillets
   Lemon Dumplings (see
   recipe, page 91)
   ● ● ●
2 cups Fish Stock (see
   recipe, page 88)
1 16-ounce can tomatoes,
   cut up
2 medium carrots, sliced
   (1 cup)
2 stalks celery, sliced
   (1 cup)
1 teaspoon salt
½ teaspoon dried basil,
   crushed
   ● ● ●
½ cup cold water
⅓ cup all-purpose flour
1 large cucumber, finely
   chopped (1 cup)

Thaw fish, if frozen. Remove skin from fillets and cut fillets into 1-inch pieces. Prepare dough for Lemon Dumplings; set aside.

In a 4-quart Dutch oven or kettle combine Fish Stock, *undrained* tomatoes, carrots, celery, salt, and basil. Bring mixture to boiling. Reduce heat; cover and simmer for 5 minutes.

In a screw-top jar combine water and flour. Cover and shake till smooth. Stir flour-water mixture into simmering stock; cook and stir till mixture is thickened and bubbly. Add the fish pieces to mixture. Return to boiling and add cucumber. Drop Lemon Dumpling dough from a tablespoon to make 6 mounds atop boiling soup. Reduce heat; cover and simmer for 20 minutes or till fish and dumplings are done. Serves 6.

QUICK-SOUPS
FISH AND SEAFOOD

Spinach-Fish Soup

2 cups milk
1 11-ounce can condensed cheddar cheese soup
1 10-ounce package frozen chopped spinach, thawed and well-drained
1 tablespoon worcestershire sauce
½ teaspoon salt
1 pound frozen fish fillets, thawed and cubed

In a 3-quart saucepan stir together milk, cheese soup, spinach, worcestershire sauce, and salt. Bring to boiling; add fish. Reduce heat; cover and simmer about 10 minutes or till fish is done. Makes 4 servings.

Speedy Clam Chowder

4 slices bacon
¼ cup chopped onion
1 10¾-ounce can condensed cream of potato soup
1 7½-ounce can minced clams
½ cup milk
Paprika

In saucepan cook bacon till crisp. Drain, reserving 2 tablespoons drippings in pan. Crumble bacon and set aside. Cook onion in reserved drippings until tender. Stir in potato soup, *undrained* clams, and milk. Simmer, uncovered, 5 to 10 minutes; stir occasionally. Stir in bacon; sprinkle with paprika. Makes 3 servings.

Salmon-Potato Chowder

This quick-to-fix salmon soup is pictured on page 33—

2 cups milk
1 10¾-ounce can condensed cream of potato soup
½ of a 10-ounce package (1 cup) frozen peas
1 16-ounce can salmon, drained, flaked, and skin and bones removed
1 cup shredded American cheese (4 ounces)
¼ teaspoon salt
⅛ teaspoon pepper

In 3-quart saucepan stir the milk into the cream of potato soup. Stir in the frozen peas. Bring mixture to boiling. Reduce heat; cover and simmer for 5 minutes. Add salmon, shredded cheese, salt, and pepper. Heat, stirring gently, till cheese melts and soup is heated through. Makes 4 servings.

Kitchen Shelf Bouillabaisse

1 7½-ounce can crab meat
1 16-ounce can tomatoes, cut up
1½ cups clam juice
1 6½- or 7-ounce can water-pack tuna, drained and flaked
½ cup dry white wine
1 tablespoon minced dried onion
1 teaspoon dried parsley flakes
1 teaspoon worcestershire sauce
¼ teaspoon dried thyme, crushed
¼ teaspoon garlic powder
5 slices French bread, toasted
Grated parmesan cheese

Drain crab meat, reserving liquid. Break meat into chunks, discarding any cartilage. In a large saucepan combine the crab, reserved crab liquid, *undrained* tomatoes, clam juice, tuna, white wine, dried onion, parsley flakes, worcestershire sauce, thyme, and garlic powder. Bring mixture to boiling. Reduce heat and simmer, uncovered, for 10 minutes. Ladle into soup bowls; top each serving with a slice of toasted French bread. Pass grated parmesan cheese to sprinkle atop. Makes 5 servings.

Corn and Clam Chowder

Bacon flavors this colorful, easy-to-fix chowder—

4 slices bacon
1 medium onion, chopped (½ cup)
2 tablespoons all-purpose flour
2 cups milk
• • •
1 16-ounce can mixed vegetables, drained
2 7½-ounce cans minced clams
1 8½-ounce can cream-style corn
½ teaspoon salt
¼ teaspoon pepper

In a 3-quart saucepan cook bacon till crisp. Drain, reserving 1 tablespoon drippings in pan. Crumble bacon and set aside.

In the same pan cook onion in reserved bacon drippings till tender but not brown. Stir in the flour. Add the milk all at once; cook and stir till the mixture is thickened and bubbly.

Stir in the mixed vegetables, *undrained* clams, cream-style corn, salt, and pepper. Heat through. Garnish soup with the crumbled bacon. Makes 6 servings.

Quick Fish Chowder

3 slices bacon
4 cups frozen fried hash brown potatoes (16 ounces)
1 cup water
1 medium onion, chopped (½ cup)
1 10¾-ounce can condensed cream of shrimp soup
1 pound frozen fish fillets, thawed and diced
3 cups milk
¼ cup snipped parsley
1 teaspoon salt
¼ teaspoon dried thyme, crushed
Paprika
Butter *or* margarine (optional)

In saucepan cook bacon till crisp, drain, reserving drippings in pan. Crumble bacon and set aside. Add frozen hash brown potatoes, water, and chopped onion to bacon drippings in pan; bring to boiling. Reduce heat; cover and simmer about 10 minutes or till vegetables are tender. Blend in cream of shrimp soup. Stir in the diced fish; cook about 15 minutes longer or till fish is done. Stir in milk, snipped parsley, salt, and thyme; heat through.

To serve, sprinkle each serving with some of the crumbled bacon and a little paprika. Top with a pat of butter or margarine, if desired. Makes 6 servings.

Crab Chowder

You'd never believe such an elegant soup is so easy to make—

1 10-ounce package frozen cauliflower
2 cups milk
2 tablespoons sliced green onion
2 tablespoons diced pimiento
½ teaspoon salt
1 cup light cream
3 tablespoons all-purpose flour
1 7½-ounce can crab meat, drained, cartilage removed, and cut up
1 3-ounce package cream cheese, cubed

In 3-quart saucepan cook cauliflower according to package directions; *do not drain.* Cut up any large pieces. Stir in milk, sliced green onion, pimiento, and salt. Heat and stir *just* till boiling.

Combine the light cream and flour; add to hot milk mixture. Cook and stir till thickened and bubbly. Add crab meat and cubed cream cheese; heat and stir till cream cheese melts and soup is heated through. Season to taste with some additional salt and pepper. Makes 4 servings.

VEGETABLES

Vegetarian Chili

Sprinkle individual servings of this meatless chili with cubes of cheese. It's pictured on page 33—

1 cup dry pinto beans
4 cups water
1 16-ounce can whole kernel corn
1 15-ounce can tomato sauce
1 large onion, chopped (1 cup)
1 4-ounce can green chili peppers, rinsed, seeded, and chopped
1 tablespoon chili powder
1 teaspoon salt
1 teaspoon dried oregano, crushed
1 clove garlic, minced
1 bay leaf
• • •
2 cups cubed cheddar *or* monterey jack cheese (8 ounces)

Rinse beans. In large saucepan combine beans and the water. Bring to boiling; reduce heat and simmer 2 minutes. Remove from heat. Cover; let stand 1 hour. (Or, soak beans in the water overnight in a covered pan.) *Do not drain.*

In a large saucepan combine pinto beans with liquid, *undrained* corn, tomato sauce, onion, chopped chili peppers, chili powder, salt, oregano, garlic, and bay leaf. Bring to boiling. Reduce heat; cover and simmer for 2 to 2½ hours. Remove bay leaf. Ladle chili into individual serving bowls. Sprinkle each serving with cheddar or monterey jack cheese cubes. Serve immediately. Makes 6 to 8 servings.

Black Bean Soup

1 pound dry black beans
8 cups water
1 large onion, finely chopped (1 cup)
2 medium carrots, finely chopped (1 cup)
2 cloves garlic, minced
¼ cup butter *or* margarine
1 16-ounce can tomatoes, cut up
2 tablespoons worcestershire sauce
2 teaspoons salt
¼ teaspoon pepper
1 bay leaf
2 hard-cooked eggs, sliced

Rinse beans. In large saucepan combine beans and water. Bring to boiling; reduce heat and simmer 2 minutes. Remove from heat. Cover; let stand 1 hour. (Or, soak beans in the water overnight in a covered pan.) *Do not drain.*

In 4-quart Dutch oven or kettle cook onion, carrots, and garlic in butter or margarine till onion is tender. Stir in beans and liquid, *undrained* tomatoes, worcestershire, salt, pepper, and bay leaf. Cover and simmer 2½ to 3 hours or till beans are done. Remove bay leaf. Mash beans slightly. Top with egg slices. Makes 8 to 10 servings.

Crockery cooking directions: Use ingredients as listed above. In saucepan combine beans and water. Bring to boiling; reduce heat and simmer for 1½ hours. Pour beans and liquid into a bowl; cover and chill.

Drain beans; reserve liquid. In electric slow crockery cooker combine beans with remaining ingredients, except eggs. Add enough reserved bean liquid to cover solids (about 2¼ cups). Cover and cook on low-heat setting 12 to 14 hours. Remove bay leaf. Mash beans slightly. Top with egg slices.

Ham and Bean Vegetable Soup

1 pound dry navy beans (2½ cups)
8 cups water
1½ pounds meaty smoked pork hocks (ham hocks)
2 medium potatoes, peeled and cubed (2 cups)
2 medium carrots, chopped (1 cup)
2 stalks celery, sliced (1 cup)
1 medium onion, chopped (½ cup)
¾ teaspoon dried thyme, crushed
½ teaspoon salt
¼ teaspoon pepper
Several dashes bottled hot pepper sauce

Rinse beans. In 4-quart Dutch oven combine beans and the water. Bring to boiling; reduce heat and simmer 2 minutes. Remove from heat. Cover; let stand 1 hour. (Or, soak beans in the water overnight in a covered pan.) *Do not drain.*

Bring beans and liquid to boiling. Add smoked pork hocks. Reduce heat; cover and simmer for 1 hour or till beans are nearly tender. Remove pork hocks. When hocks are cool enough to handle, cut off meat and coarsely chop. Discard bones. Return meat to pan. Add potatoes, carrots, celery, onion, thyme, salt, pepper, and hot pepper sauce. Cover and simmer 30 minutes or till vegetables are tender. Season to taste with salt and pepper. Makes 8 to 10 servings.

Ham and Bean Vegetable Soup

Country-Style Bean Soup

Pork sausage adds extra flavor to this lima bean soup—

1 pound dry lima beans (2½ cups)
8 cups water
1 teaspoon salt
• • •
8 ounces bulk pork sausage
2 medium apples, peeled and cubed (2 cups)
1 large onion, chopped (1 cup)
2 stalks celery, chopped (1 cup)
1 clove garlic, minced
1 28-ounce can tomatoes, cut up
2 tablespoons brown sugar
2 tablespoons prepared mustard
1 teaspoon salt
¼ teaspoon pepper

Rinse beans. In 5-quart Dutch oven or kettle combine beans and the water. Bring to boiling. Reduce heat; cover and simmer 2 minutes. Remove from heat. Cover; let stand 1 hour. (Or, soak beans in the water overnight in a covered pan.) *Do not drain.* Add 1 teaspoon salt. Bring to boiling. Reduce heat; cover and simmer the beans 1 hour.

In a skillet cook pork sausage with apples, onion, celery, and garlic till sausage is done; spoon off fat. Stir sausage mixture into the beans. Stir in the *undrained* tomatoes, brown sugar, mustard, 1 teaspoon salt, and the pepper. Cover and simmer 1 hour longer. Serve in bowls. Makes 8 to 10 servings.

Vegetable Soup with Basil Pistou

8 ounces dry navy beans (1¼ cups)
7 cups water
1 10¾-ounce can *condensed* chicken broth
2 teaspoons salt
⅛ teaspoon pepper
1 large onion, chopped (1 cup)
½ cup diced salt pork (4 ounces)
2 potatoes, peeled and diced
2 medium carrots, diced
2 small zucchini, sliced
2 small tomatoes, peeled and chopped
1½ cups coarsely chopped cabbage
1 cup bias-sliced green beans
1 cup fresh shelled lima beans *or* ½ of a 10-ounce package frozen lima beans
1 medium turnip, peeled and diced (1 cup)
½ cup chopped celery
3 cups lightly packed fresh basil leaves, snipped
1 cup grated gruyère cheese (4 ounces)
2 cloves garlic
1 teaspoon lemon juice
¼ teaspoon salt
½ cup olive oil

Rinse beans. In 5-quart Dutch oven combine beans, water, broth, the 2 teaspoons salt, and the pepper. Bring to boiling; reduce heat and simmer 2 minutes. Remove from heat. Cover; let stand 1 hour. (Or, add water, broth, salt, and pepper to beans. Cover and refrigerate overnight.) *Do not drain.* Return to boiling; cover and simmer 1½ hours.

In a skillet cook onion and salt pork till pork is brown. Add to beans. Stir in potatoes, carrots, zucchini, to-matoes, cabbage, green beans, lima beans, turnip, and celery. Bring to boiling. Reduce heat; cover and simmer 30 to 40 minutes or till vegetables are just tender.

To make pistou, place basil, gruyère cheese, garlic, lemon juice, and the ¼ teaspoon salt in blender container. Cover and blend till smooth. (Or, place in mortar; pound with pestle to a smooth paste.) Add olive oil, a teaspoon at a time, till the mixture is consistency of soft butter.

To serve, ladle soup into bowls. Pass pistou to stir into each serving. Makes 10 servings.

Potato-Cheese Soup

3 medium potatoes, peeled and cut up
1 small onion, finely chopped (⅓ cup)
Milk
3 tablespoons butter *or* margarine, melted
2 tablespoons all-purpose flour
2 tablespoons snipped parsley
¾ teaspoon salt
Dash pepper
1 cup shredded Swiss cheese (4 ounces)

In 2-quart saucepan add potatoes and onion to 1 cup lightly salted boiling *water.* Cover and cook about 20 minutes or till potatoes are tender. Mash potatoes slightly; do not drain. Measure mixture and add enough milk to make 5 cups. Blend melted butter, flour, parsley, salt, and pepper. Stir into potato mixture in saucepan; cook and stir till thickened and bubbly. Add cheese; cook and stir till cheese is partially melted. Serve immediately. Makes 4 or 5 servings.

Cheesy Beer-Vegetable Soup

This hearty soup combines parsnips, green pepper, corn, and mushrooms with the flavors of beer and cheese—

1 large onion, finely chopped (1 cup)
1 medium green pepper, chopped (½ cup)
2 tablespoons butter *or* margarine
2 cups chopped parsnips
1 16-ounce can whole kernel corn
2 cups chicken broth (see tip, page 87)
1 12-ounce can beer
1 4-ounce can mushroom stems and pieces
½ teaspoon dry mustard
⅓ cup cold water
3 tablespoons all-purpose flour
2 cups shredded American cheese (8 ounces)

In 3-quart saucepan cook onion and green pepper in butter or margarine till tender but not brown. Add parsnips, *undrained* corn, chicken broth, beer, *undrained* mushrooms, and mustard. Bring to boiling. Reduce heat; cover and simmer 20 to 30 minutes or till parsnips are done.

In screw-top jar combine water and flour. Cover; shake till thoroughly mixed. Stir into hot vegetable mixture. Cook and stir till slightly thickened and bubbly. Stir in the shredded cheese. Continue heating and stirring till cheese is melted. Makes 6 servings.

Big-Meal Soup

1 pound dry green *or* yellow split peas
7 cups water
1 1-pound ham bone *or* 1 pound smoked pork hocks (ham hocks)
2 medium carrots, coarsely chopped (1 cup)
1 medium onion, chopped (½ cup)
1 teaspoon salt
1 16-ounce can tomatoes, cut up
1 medium green pepper, chopped (½ cup)
1 stalk celery, chopped (½ cup)

Rinse peas. In 4-quart Dutch oven combine first 6 ingredients. Bring to boiling. Reduce heat; cover and simmer for 45 to 60 minutes or till peas are tender. Remove ham bone and cut off meat. Discard bone.

Press *half* the pea mixture through a sieve. (Or, process in blender or food processor till smooth.) Return to Dutch oven. Stir in meat. Add *undrained* tomatoes, green pepper, and celery. Simmer 15 to 20 minutes or till celery and green pepper are done. Season to taste with salt and pepper. Makes 6 to 8 servings.

Soaking Dry Beans

Dry beans and dry whole peas need soaking before cooking, but split peas and lentils do not. Rinse and drain all the dried products before cooking.

To soak, combine dry beans with the specified amount of water in Dutch oven. Bring to boiling. Reduce heat; simmer 2 minutes. Remove from heat. Cover; let stand 1 hour. Or, soak beans in water overnight.

Curry-Vegetable Soup

Buttermilk adds a tangy flavor to this spicy bean soup—

1 pound dry baby lima beans (2½ cups)
8 cups water
1 large onion, chopped (1 cup)
1 tablespoon instant chicken bouillon granules
• • •
2 cups cauliflowerets *or* 1 10-ounce package frozen cauliflower
2 medium apples, peeled and chopped (2 cups)
2 medium carrots, sliced (1 cup)
1 tablespoon curry powder
1½ teaspoons salt
¼ teaspoon ground cardamom
• • •
4 beaten egg yolks
2 cups buttermilk
Snipped parsley

Rinse beans. In a Dutch oven or kettle combine beans and the water. Bring to boiling. Reduce heat; simmer 2 minutes. Remove from heat. Cover; let stand 1 hour. (Or, soak beans in the water overnight in a covered pan.) *Do not drain.* Add onion and bouillon granules to beans. Cover and simmer 1 hour or till beans are nearly tender.

Add cauliflowerets, apples, carrots, curry, salt, and cardamom. Simmer the mixture 30 to 40 minutes more or till vegetables are tender. Combine beaten egg yolks and buttermilk; add to soup. Heat through; do not boil. Serve in soup bowls. Sprinkle with parsley. Makes 8 servings.

Pinto Bean Gumbo

1⅔ cups dry pinto beans
  or dry navy beans
7 cups water
1 large onion, chopped
  (1 cup)
½ cup diced salt pork
  (4 ounces)
½ teaspoon salt
1 bay leaf
2 cups fresh okra, thinly
  sliced
1 16-ounce can tomatoes,
  cut up
1 12-ounce can whole kernel
  corn, drained
2 teaspoons worcestershire
  sauce
1 teaspoon salt
1 teaspoon sugar
1 teaspoon dried thyme,
  crushed
½ teaspoon bottled hot
  pepper sauce

Rinse beans. In 5-quart Dutch oven or kettle combine beans and the water. Bring to boiling. Reduce heat; cover and simmer 2 minutes. Remove from heat. Cover; let stand 1 hour. (Or, soak beans in the water overnight in a covered pan.) *Do not drain.*

Add onion, salt pork, the ½ teaspoon salt, and the bay leaf to beans and liquid. Bring to boiling. Reduce heat; cover and simmer 2 to 2½ hours or till beans are tender. Add sliced okra, *undrained* tomatoes, drained corn, worcestershire sauce, the 1 teaspoon salt, sugar, thyme, and bottled hot pepper sauce. Simmer the mixture 30 minutes or till okra is tender. Remove bay leaf before serving. Makes 10 servings.

Pinto Bean Gumbo
Onion Supper Soup

Onion Supper Soup

3 large onions, thinly
  sliced
1 clove garlic, minced
¼ cup butter *or* margarine
4 cups Vegetable Stock (see
  recipe, page 88) *or*
  Browned Beef Stock (see
  recipe, page 85)
4 thick slices French bread
4 ounces Swiss *or* gruyère
  cheese, sliced
  Grated parmesan cheese

In covered saucepan cook onions and garlic in butter over low heat 20 minutes or till very tender; stir occasionally. Add stock and ¼ teaspoon *pepper.* Bring to boiling; cover and simmer 15 minutes. Meanwhile, toast bread. Arrange slices on baking sheet. Top each with sliced cheese; sprinkle with parmesan. Broil 2 to 3 minutes or till cheese melts. Ladle soup into 4 bowls. Top each with a toast slice. Makes 4 servings.

Bean-Bacon Chowder

6 slices bacon, cut up
1 cup chopped onion
2 tablespoons all-purpose
  flour
3 cups milk
2 medium potatoes, peeled
¼ teaspoon dried thyme,
  crushed
1 22-ounce jar baked beans
¼ cup snipped parsley

In saucepan cook bacon and onion till bacon is lightly browned and onion is tender. Blend in flour. Add milk; cook and stir till bubbly. Dice potatoes; add with thyme, 1 teaspoon *salt,* and ⅛ teaspoon *pepper.* Cover; simmer 12 to 15 minutes or till potatoes are done. Stir in beans; heat through. Top with parsley. Serves 6.

Minestrone

1½ cups dry navy beans
9 cups water
2 medium carrots, chopped
  (1 cup)
6 slices bacon
1 large onion, chopped
  (1 cup)
2 stalks celery, chopped
  (1 cup)
1 clove garlic, minced
2 16-ounce cans tomatoes,
  cut up
2 cups finely shredded
  cabbage
2 medium zucchini, sliced
  (about 2 cups)
2 teaspoons salt
1 teaspoon dried basil,
  crushed
½ teaspoon ground sage
¼ teaspoon pepper
3 ounces fine noodles (1½
  cups) *or* ½ recipe
  Whole Wheat Noodles
  (see recipe, page 89)

Rinse beans. In Dutch oven or kettle combine beans and the water. Bring to boiling; reduce heat and simmer 2 minutes. Remove from heat. Cover; let stand 1 hour. (Or, soak beans in the water overnight in a covered pan.) *Do not drain.* Add carrots. Cover and simmer 2½ to 3 hours.

Meanwhile, in a skillet cook bacon till crisp. Drain, reserving 2 tablespoons drippings. Crumble bacon; set aside. Cook onion, celery, and garlic in reserved drippings till vegetables are almost tender; drain. Add to beans along with *undrained* tomatoes, cabbage, zucchini, salt, basil, sage, and pepper. Bring to boiling; stir in noodles. Reduce heat and simmer 20 to 25 minutes more or till noodles are tender. Stir in crumbled bacon. Top each serving with grated parmesan cheese, if desired. Makes 8 servings.

Lentil-Pepperoni Soup

Serve this stick-to-the-ribs soup with bulgur wheat, also called cracked wheat. See it on page 44—

1½ cups dry lentils
4 ounces pepperoni, thinly sliced and halved
1 medium onion, chopped (½ cup)
1 6-ounce can tomato paste
1½ teaspoons salt
¼ teaspoon dried oregano, crushed
¼ teaspoon ground sage
⅛ teaspoon cayenne
2 medium tomatoes, peeled and cut up
1 medium carrot, thinly sliced (½ cup)
1 stalk celery, sliced (½ cup)
½ cup bulgur wheat

Rinse lentils; in Dutch oven combine with 6 cups *water*, pepperoni, onion, tomato paste, salt, oregano, sage, and cayenne. Bring to boiling. Reduce heat; cover and simmer for 30 minutes, stirring occasionally. Add tomatoes, carrot, and celery; cover and simmer 40 minutes longer.

Meanwhile, cook bulgur according to package directions. Mound bulgur in soup. Makes 6 to 8 servings.

Crockery cooking directions: Use ingredients as listed above. Rinse lentils. In large saucepan combine 5 cups *water* and lentils; bring to boiling. Reduce heat; cover and simmer 30 minutes. *Do not drain.* In electric slow crockery cooker combine lentils and their liquid with remaining ingredients, except bulgur. Cover and cook on low-heat setting for 10 hours. Cook bulgur according to package directions. Stir soup before serving; serve as directed above.

Spicy Eggplant Parmesan Stew

2 slices bacon
1 medium eggplant, peeled and cubed (5 cups)
1 medium onion, chopped (½ cup)
1 clove garlic, minced
1½ cups beef broth (see tip, page 87)
1 8-ounce can tomato sauce
½ teaspoon dried oregano, crushed
¼ teaspoon salt
⅛ teaspoon crushed dried red pepper
• • •
6 ounces mozzarella cheese, sliced
¼ cup grated parmesan cheese (1 ounce)

In a 3-quart saucepan cook bacon till crisp. Drain, reserving bacon drippings in pan. Crumble bacon and set aside for garnish.

In the reserved bacon drippings cook the cubed eggplant, chopped onion, and minced garlic, covered, over low heat till eggplant is golden, stirring occasionally. Stir in the beef broth, tomato sauce, oregano, salt, and crushed red pepper. Bring mixture to boiling. Reduce heat; cover and simmer about 15 minutes or till the eggplant is tender.

Spoon the eggplant mixture into 4 individual casseroles. Top each casserole with sliced mozzarella cheese; sprinkle with the grated parmesan cheese. Place under broiler; broil till cheese melts. Garnish with the reserved bacon. Makes 4 servings.

Italian Bean Soup

1 cup dry navy beans
1 8-ounce can tomato sauce
1 cup chopped onion
1 cup chopped carrots
½ cup chopped green pepper
2 cloves garlic, minced
2 tablespoons instant beef bouillon granules
1½ teaspoons *each* dried basil, crushed, *and* dried oregano, crushed
½ cup macaroni

Rinse beans; add 8 cups *water*. Boil 2 minutes. Remove from heat; cover and let stand 1 hour. (Or, soak in the water overnight.) *Do not drain.* Stir in 1 teaspoon *salt* and remaining ingredients, except macaroni. Cover, simmer 1½ hours. Stir in macaroni; cook, uncovered, 10 to 15 minutes. Makes 6 to 8 servings.

Mexican Red Bean and Pineapple Soup

1 cup chopped onion
½ cup chopped green pepper
1 clove garlic, minced
1 tablespoon cooking oil
2 16-ounce cans red kidney beans
1 16-ounce can tomatoes, cut up
½ cup diced fully cooked ham
1 bay leaf
¼ teaspoon *each* ground cumin, ground cinnamon, *and* dried oregano, crushed
1 8¼-ounce can crushed pineapple

Cook onion, green pepper, and garlic in oil till tender. Stir in 1 teaspoon *salt* and remaining ingredients, except pineapple. Cover; simmer 30 minutes. Stir in *undrained* pineapple; heat through. Serves 4 to 6.

QUICK-SOUPS

VEGETABLES

Butter Bean Soup

½ pound bulk pork sausage
¼ cup sliced green onion
3 16-ounce cans butter beans
2 cups milk
1 10¾-ounce can condensed
   tomato soup
1 teaspoon salt
½ teaspoon dried thyme,
   crushed
   Dash pepper

In large saucepan cook sausage and onion till sausage is done. Drain off fat. To sausage add *undrained* beans, milk, soup, salt, thyme, and pepper. Heat to boiling. Reduce heat; cover and simmer 10 minutes. Top with more sliced green onions, if desired. Serves 6.

Cheese-Bean Chowder

2 12-ounce cans whole kernel
   corn with *sweet* peppers
1 16-ounce can red kidney
   beans, drained
1½ cups milk
¾ teaspoon chili powder
½ teaspoon salt
1 6-ounce roll cheese food
   with hickory smoke
   flavor, cut up

In 3-quart saucepan combine *undrained* corn, the beans, milk, chili powder, and salt. Cook, stirring occasionally, over medium-low heat till just bubbly. Add cheese; heat and stir till cheese melts and soup is hot. Serves 4.

Black-Eyed Pea and Rice Stew

Patterned after the Southern favorite "Hopping John," this stew is delicious served with corn bread—

2 15-ounce cans black-eyed
   peas
3 cups water
1 large onion, sliced
2 stalks celery, sliced
   (1 cup)
2 slices bacon, diced
1 teaspoon instant chicken
   bouillon granules
½ teaspoon garlic salt
¼ teaspoon pepper
¼ teaspoon bottled hot
   pepper sauce
½ cup long grain rice

In a large saucepan stir together the *undrained* black-eyed peas, the water, sliced onion, sliced celery, diced bacon, chicken bouillon granules, garlic salt, pepper, and bottled hot pepper sauce. Bring mixture to boiling. Stir in the uncooked rice. Reduce heat; cover and simmer for 20 to 25 minutes or till the rice is done. Makes 4 servings.

Egg-Corn Chowder

4 hard-cooked eggs
1 17-ounce can cream-style
   corn
2 cups milk
1 green pepper, finely
   chopped (½ cup)
1 tablespoon minced dried
   onion
1 tablespoon prepared
   mustard
¾ teaspoon salt

Remove yolks from *two* eggs; set aside. Chop remaining eggs and whites. In saucepan combine chopped eggs with remaining ingredients. Cover; simmer 15 minutes. Sieve reserved yolks atop. Serves 4.

Cabbage-Cheese Soup

3½ cups milk
1 10¾-ounce can condensed
   cream of potato soup
2 cups coarsely chopped
   cabbage
1 medium carrot, coarsely
   shredded (½ cup)
1 cup shredded process Swiss
   cheese (4 ounces)
½ teaspoon caraway seed
¼ teaspoon pepper

In saucepan stir milk into soup. Cook and stir till bubbly; stir in cabbage and carrot. Cover and simmer 5 minutes or till cabbage is done. Stir in cheese, caraway, and pepper. Heat and stir till cheese melts. Makes 4 servings.

SOUP~MAKING BASICS

stocks~noodles~ dumplings~croutons and crackers

Here's everything you need to know to make soups and stews from scratch, including shortcuts to home-style flavor.

A good stock is the basis of a great soup. You can make one by simmering meat bones, vegetables, and seasonings in a stockpot. You'll find recipes for beef, chicken, veal, vegetable, and fish stocks, as well as one that uses vegetable leftovers and your choice of meat bones.

Crown your soup with your choice of noodles, dumplings, or croutons. Or, serve with crackers you make yourself.

STOCKS

Beef Stock

Try making Browned Beef Stock when you want a stock with a richer, browned flavor—

6 pounds beef soup bones (neck bones, arm bones, shank bones, or marrow bones)
1 large onion, sliced
2 carrots, cut up
2 stalks celery with leaves, cut up
1 large tomato, cut up (optional)
8 whole black peppercorns
4 sprigs parsley
1 bay leaf
1 clove garlic, halved
1 tablespoon salt
12 cups cold water

In a large stockpot or Dutch oven place beef soup bones; onion; carrots; celery; tomato, if desired; peppercorns; parsley; bay leaf; garlic; and salt. Add the water. Bring to boiling. Reduce heat; cover and simmer for 4 to 5 hours.

Lift out beef bones with a slotted spoon. Strain the stock through a sieve lined with 1 or 2 layers of cheesecloth; discard the seasonings. Clarify stock, if desired

◆→ Clarifying ◆→

Clarify beef stock, chicken stock, or white stock when you want a clear soup. Clarifying removes solid flecks that are too small to be strained out with cheesecloth, but which will muddy a soup's appearance.

To clarify, stir together ¼ cup cold water, 1 egg white, and 1 egg shell, crushed. Add to strained stock; bring to boiling. Remove from heat and let stand 5 minutes. Strain again through a sieve lined with cheesecloth.

(see tip, above).

Skim off the fat with a metal spoon, or chill the stock and lift off the solidified fat. Makes about 10 cups stock.

Browned Beef Stock: Use ingredients as listed above. Spread beef bones, onion slices, and carrots in a large shallow roasting pan so that the beef bones will brown evenly. Bake the bones in a 450° oven about 30 minutes or till the

◆→ Stock Making ◆→

- It's not necessary to peel or trim vegetables for stocks, since they will be strained out. Just wash and cut them up.
- Start with cold water to extract the most flavor from meat and vegetables.
- Simmer stocks slowly for best flavor—bubbles should form slowly and burst before reaching the surface.
- To avoid spills, ladle stock into the strainer rather than pouring it.
- Avoid over-seasoning stocks for other recipes.

bones are well browned, turning occasionally with tongs. Drain off any fat.

In a large stockpot or Dutch oven place the browned bones, onion, and carrots. Add the celery; tomato, if desired; peppercorns; parsley; bay leaf; garlic; and salt. Add the water. Bring to boiling. Reduce heat; cover and simmer for 4 to 5 hours.

Strain, clarify, and remove fat as directed above.

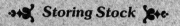
Ladle the finished stock into pint or quart jars or other non-plastic containers while it is still hot. Cover and refrigerate to chill quickly. If you are saving the meat for another use, store it in a separate container from the stock for easy use.

Stock may be stored in the refrigerator for a few days, or in the freezer for up to 6 months. Be sure to label the contents of each container with the type of stock, quantity, and the date.

If you frequently use stock in small quantities, freeze it in ice cube trays. When frozen, place frozen stock cubes in a plastic bag and return them to the freezer. Measure the volume of a melted cube to determine the exact amount of stock in each cube (approximately 2 tablespoons).

stocks (continued)

Basic Stock

Use strong-flavored vegetables with the beef or ham bones; more delicate ones with chicken pieces—

    4 pounds meaty beef bones or
       2½ pounds chicken necks,
       wings, and backs or
       2 pounds meaty ham bones
    3 medium onions, quartered
 1½ cups celery leaves
    6 sprigs parsley
    4 whole black peppercorns
    2 or 3 bay leaves
    1 or 2 cloves garlic, halved
    1 tablespoon salt*
    1 tablespoon dried basil,
       crushed or 2 teaspoons
       dried thyme, crushed
  10 cups cold water
Choose 2 or 3 of the following:
 1½ cups potato peelings
 1½ cups carrot peelings
 1½ cups turnip leaves or
       peelings
 1½ cups parsnip leaves or
       peelings
    4 or 5 outer cabbage leaves
   ¾ cup sliced green onion
       tops
   ¾ cup sliced leek tops

In a 10-quart stockpot or Dutch oven place the beef bones, chicken pieces, or ham bones. Add the quartered onions, celery leaves, parsley, whole peppercorns, bay leaves, garlic, salt, and basil or thyme. Add the cold water. Choose 2 or 3 of the vegetable peelings, leaves, or tops. Add these to the stockpot or Dutch oven.

Bring mixture to boiling. Reduce heat; cover and simmer over low heat for about 3 hours. Lift out the meat bones with a slotted spoon; set aside.

Strain the stock by ladling it through a sieve lined with 1 or 2 layers of cheesecloth; discard vegetables and seasonings. Clarify the stock, if desired (see tip on page 85). Skim off the excess fat with a metal spoon, or chill the stock and lift off the solidified fat.

When bones are cool enough to handle, remove meat from bones; reserve meat for another use, if desired. Discard bones. Store the stock and any leftover meat in separate covered containers in the refrigerator or freezer. Makes 7 to 8 cups stock.

*Reduce salt to 1 teaspoon when using ham bones, then season finished stock to taste.

Chicken Stock

2 pounds bony chicken
    pieces (backs, necks,
    and wings)
3 stalks celery with
    leaves, cut up
2 medium carrots, cut up
1½ teaspoons salt
¼ teaspoon pepper
6 cups water
1 large onion, cut into
    thirds
3 whole cloves

In a 5-quart stockpot or Dutch oven
combine chicken pieces, celery,
carrots, salt, and pepper; add water.
Stud each onion third with a whole
clove. Add to pot. Bring to boiling.
Reduce heat; cover and simmer
about 1 hour or till chicken is tender.
    Lift out chicken pieces with a
slotted spoon. Strain stock through
a sieve lined with 1 or 2 layers of
cheesecloth; discard vegetables.
    Clarify stock, if desired (see tip on
page 85). Skim off fat with a metal
spoon, or chill stock and lift off the
solidified fat.
    When chicken is cool enough to
handle, remove chicken from bones
and save meat for another use, if
desired. Makes 5 cups stock.
    Crockery cooking directions: Use
ingredients as listed above *except*
decrease water to *4 cups.*
    In an electric slow crockery cooker
place chicken, celery, carrots, salt,
and pepper. Add 4 cups water. Stud
each onion third with a whole clove;
add to cooker. Cover and cook on
low-heat setting for 8 to 10 hours.
Remove chicken and vegetables
from crockery cooker with a slotted
spoon. Strain and clarify stock;
remove fat as directed above. Makes
about 4½ cups stock

➸✖ Stock Substitutions ✖➔•

When a recipe calls for beef or
chicken broth, use one of the
stock recipes in this chapter.
Or, if you're in a hurry, you
don't need to start from
scratch. Excellent commercial
substitutes are available. And,
if you don't have the specified
flavor, substitute a different
one—you may even prefer it!
    Canned beef and chicken
broths are ready to use straight
from the can. Canned
condensed beef and chicken
broths are also available. These
must be diluted according to
can directions.
    Instant bouillon granules and
cubes can be purchased in beef,
chicken, vegetable, and onion
flavors. These should be mixed
with water according to package directions before using as a
broth substitute.

stocks (continued)

Vegetable Stock

- 2 tablespoons butter *or* margarine
- 3 carrots, chopped
- 2 stalks celery with leaves, chopped
- 1 large onion, chopped
- 1 turnip, chopped
- 1 clove garlic, halved
- ½ teaspoon dried thyme, crushed
- 2 tomatoes, cut up
- 1 cup shredded lettuce
- 2 sprigs parsley
- 1½ teaspoons salt
- ¼ teaspoon pepper

In large saucepan melt butter. Add carrots, celery, onion, turnip, garlic, and thyme. Cover and cook over low heat 30 minutes or till vegetables are tender, stirring occasionally. Add remaining ingredients and 6 cups cold *water*. Bring to boiling. Reduce heat; cover and simmer 2 hours. Strain; discard vegetables. Makes 4½ cups.

White Stock

- 4 pounds veal knuckle, cut up
- 2 stalks celery with leaves, cut up
- 2 medium carrots, cut up
- 1 tablespoon salt
- 1 large onion, quartered
- 4 whole cloves
- 2 sprigs parsley
- 1 clove garlic, halved
- 1 small bay leaf
- 1 teaspoon dried thyme, crushed

In stockpot or Dutch oven place veal, celery, carrots, and salt. Stud each onion quarter with a clove; add to pot. To make a *bouquet garni*, place parsley, garlic, bay leaf, and thyme on an 8-inch square of cheesecloth. Bring up edges and tie with thread; add to pot. Add 10 cups cold *water*. Cover and simmer 5 hours. Remove *bouquet garni* and veal; discard. Strain stock; clarify, if desired (see tip on page 85). Skim fat, or chill and lift off fat. Makes 9½ cups stock.

Crockery cooking directions: Use ingredients as listed above, *except* use only 2½ to 3 pounds veal knuckle. In slow electric crockery cooker place 2½ to 3 pounds veal knuckle, celery, carrots, and salt. Stud each onion quarter with a clove; add to cooker. Make *bouquet garni* as above; add to cooker. Add 6 to 6½ cups *water*. Cover; cook on low-heat setting 12 to 15 hours. Strain, clarify, and remove fat. Makes 6 cups.

Fish Stock

- 1½ pounds fresh *or* frozen dressed fish (with head and tail)
- 1 small onion, chopped
- 1 stalk celery with leaves, chopped
- 3 sprigs parsley
- ½ lemon, sliced
- 1 teaspoon salt
- 3 whole black peppercorns
- 3 whole cloves

Cut up fish, if necessary, to fit in a large saucepan. Add the onion, celery, parsley, lemon, salt, peppercorns and cloves. Add 6 cups cold *water*. Bring to boiling. Reduce heat; cover and simmer 30 minutes. Strain through sieve lined with 1 or 2 layers of cheesecloth. Reserve fish for another use; discard skin, bones, and seasonings. Makes 4 cups.

NOODLES

Homemade Noodles

Use these in any recipe that calls for noodles. Or, substitute packaged or frozen noodles, following the cooking directions on the package—

1 beaten egg
2 tablespoons milk
½ teaspoon salt
1 cup all-purpose flour

In mixing bowl combine egg, milk, and salt. Stir in enough of the flour to make a stiff dough. Cover and let rest for 10 minutes.

On floured surface roll dough to a 16x12-inch rectangle. Let stand 20 minutes. Roll up loosely; cut into ¼-inch slices. Unroll; cut into desired lengths. Spread out and let dry on rack 2 hours. Store in airtight container till ready to use.

Cook noodles as directed in recipe, or drop into a large amount of boiling salted water or soup. Cook, uncovered, 10 to 12 minutes. Makes about 3 cups.

Whole Wheat Noodles: Prepare as directed above, *except* substitute ½ cup *whole wheat flour* for ½ cup of the all-purpose flour.

Puffy Cheese Noodles

1 beaten egg
1 tablespoon milk
¾ cup all-purpose flour
¼ cup grated parmesan cheese
1 teaspoon baking powder

Green Noodles

1¼ cups torn spinach leaves
2 tablespoons water
1 egg
½ teaspoon salt
1¼ cups all-purpose flour

In saucepan combine spinach and water. Cover and cook till spinach is very tender. Cool slightly; place spinach and liquid in blender container. Add egg and salt; cover and blend till smooth. Transfer to bowl. Add enough of the flour to make a stiff dough. Knead on lightly floured surface 1 minute. Roll very thin on floured surface. Let rest 20 minutes. Roll up loosely. Slice ¼

Mix together egg and milk. In a mixing bowl stir together flour, parmesan, baking powder, and ¼ teaspoon *salt*. Stir in egg mixture to make a stiff dough.

Turn dough onto a lightly floured surface. Roll out to a 12x12-inch square. Roll up jelly roll-style; slice into ¼-inch-wide strips. Unroll. Cut into desired lengths. Use as directed in recipe, or spread out and let dry on a rack up to 2 hours. Drop noodles into boiling salted water or prepared soup. Cook, uncovered, for 10 to 12 minutes. Makes about 2½ cups.

inch wide. Unroll. Cut into desired lengths. Spread out; let dry on a rack for 2 hours. Store in airtight container till needed. Use as directed in recipe, or cook, uncovered, in boiling salted water or prepared soup for 10 to 12 minutes or till tender. Makes about 3½ cups.

DUMPLINGS

Danish Dumplings

These are made like cream puffs—

- ½ cup water
- ¼ cup butter *or* margarine
- ½ cup all-purpose flour
- 1 teaspoon baking powder
- ⅛ teaspoon salt
- 2 eggs
- 1 tablespoon snipped parsley

In a saucepan combine the water and the butter or margarine; bring to boiling. Add the flour, baking powder, and salt all at once, stirring vigorously. Cook, stirring constantly, till mixture forms a ball that doesn't separate. Remove from heat; cool slightly. Add the eggs, one at a time, beating well after each addition till mixture is smooth. Stir in the parsley.

Drop dumpling dough from a tablespoon to make 12 mounds atop bubbling soup or stew. Cover and simmer for 20 minutes (do not lift cover). Makes 12 dumplings.

Fluffy Dumplings

To keep dough from sticking to spoon, dip spoon into the hot soup or stew liquid before forming each dumpling—

- 1 cup all-purpose flour
- 2 teaspoons baking powder
- ½ teaspoon salt
- ½ cup milk
- 2 tablespoons cooking oil *or* melted shortening

In a mixing bowl thoroughly stir together the flour, baking powder, and salt. Combine the milk and the cooking oil or melted shortening; add liquid mixture all at once to the dry ingredients, stirring just till moistened.

Drop the dumpling dough from a tablespoon to make 4 to 6 mounds atop bubbling soup or stew. Cover tightly and simmer for 15 minutes (do not lift cover). Makes 4 to 6 dumplings.

Easy Dumplings

Here's an easy way to mix up delicious dumplings—

- 2 cups packaged biscuit mix
- ⅔ cup milk

In mixing bowl place biscuit mix. Add milk all at once; stir just till mixture is moistened.

Drop dough from a tablespoon to make 10 to 12 mounds atop the bubbling soup or stew. Simmer dumplings, uncovered, about 10 minutes. Cover and simmer 10 minutes longer (do not lift cover). Makes 10 to 12 dumplings.